THE
WRIGHT BROTHERS

Orville Wright flying at Tempelhof Field near Berlin, Germany, in 1909.

THE
WRIGHT BROTHERS

How They Invented the Airplane

RUSSELL FREEDMAN

With Original Photographs by Wilbur and Orville Wright

Holiday House / New York

Copyright ©1991 by Russell Freedman
Printed in the United States of America
Library of Congress Cataloging-in-Publication Data
Freedman, Russell.
The Wright brothers : how they invented the airplane / by Russell
Freedman ; with orginal photographs by Wilbur and Orville Wright.
p.   cm.
Includes bibliographical references and index.
Summary: Follows the lives of the Wright brothers and describes
how they developed the first airplane.
ISBN 0-8234-0875-2
1. Wright, Orville, 1871–1948—Juvenile literature.   2. Wright,
Wilbur, 1867–1912—Juvenile literature.   3. Aeronautics—United
States—Biography—Juvenile literature.   [1. Wright, Orville,
1871–1948.   2. Wright, Wilbur, 1867–1912.   3. Aeronautics—
Biography.]   I. Wright, Wilbur, 1867–1912, ill.   II. Wright,
Orville, 1871–1948, ill.   III. Title.
TL540.W7F69   1991
629.13′0092′2—dc20
[B]   [920]
90-48440   CIP   AC
ISBN 0-8234-0875-2
ISBN 0-8234-1082-X (pbk)

For CHARLES J. ARNOLD,
a frequent flier

All photographs not specifically credited below were furnished by Wright State University, Dayton, Ohio, and are herewith gratefully acknowledged.

Library of Congress: pages 11, 26, 31, 39, 42, 58, 59, 79, 83, 91, 111, 115.

Smithsonian Institution: pages 4, 7, 9, 14, 16, 18, 19, 21, 22, 23, 24, 25, 48, 49, 78, 79, 94, 96, 101, 106, 112, 114, 117.

Contents

THE
WRIGHT BROTHERS

The 1904 Wright Flyer over Huffman Prairie. The Wrights made their first complete circle with this machine on September 20, 1904.

ONE

What Amos Root Saw

No one had ever seen what Amos Root saw on that September afternoon in 1904. Standing in a cow pasture near Dayton, Ohio, he looked up and watched a flying machine circle in the sky above him. He could see the bold pilot lying facedown on the lower wing, staring straight ahead as he steered the craft to a landing in the grass.

The pilot was Wilbur Wright. He and his brother Orville had built the machine themselves in the workroom of their bicycle shop. Now they were testing it out at a farmer's field called Huffman Prairie.

Amos Root had come all the way down from Medina, Ohio, where he ran a beekeepers' supply house. For weeks he had heard rumors about the Wright brothers' flying machine, and being a curious fellow, he wanted to investigate this miracle for himself. So he packed a bag, climbed into his automobile, and drove nearly 200 miles to Dayton—a very long trip at a time when automobiles were still called "horseless carriages."

He was lucky enough to be on hand when Wilbur Wright took off and flew once around Huffman Prairie—the first circling flight ever made by an airplane. The flight lasted 1 minute 36 seconds.

Back home in Medina, Root wrote history's earliest eyewitness account of an airplane in controlled flight. His article appeared in the January 1, 1905, issue of *Gleanings in Bee Culture*, a magazine he published for customers of his supply house.

"Dear friends," he wrote, "I have a wonderful story to tell you—a story that, in some respects, outrivals the Arabian Nights fables." He reported that "two minister's boys who love machinery, and who are interested in the modern developments of science and art . . . began studying the flights of birds and insects. From this they turned their attention to what has been done in the way of enabling men to fly. . . . This work, mind you, was all new. Nobody living could give them any advice. It was like exploring a new and unknown domain."

Root congratulated himself on being the first to see an airplane "turn the corner and come back to the starting point." Then he described his reactions to that historic flight:

"The machine is held until ready to start by a sort of trap to be sprung when all is ready; then with a tremendous flapping and snapping of the four-cylinder engine, the huge machine springs aloft. When it first turned that circle, and came near the starting-point, I was right in front of it; and I said then, and I believe still, it was . . . the grandest sight of my life. Imagine a locomotive that has left its track and is climbing up in the air right toward you—a locomotive without any wheels, we will say, but with white wings instead . . . coming right toward you with a tremendous flap of its propellers, and you will have something like what I saw. The younger brother bade me move to one side for fear it might come down suddenly; but I tell you friends, the sensation one feels in such a crisis is something hard to describe."

Root compared the Wright brothers to another explorer of the unknown, Christopher Columbus: "When Columbus discovered America he did not know what the outcome would be, and no one at that time knew. . . . In a like manner these two brothers have probably not even a faint glimpse of what their discovery is going to bring to the children of men."

TWO

Wilbur and Orville

"From the time we were little children," Wilbur Wright once said, "my brother Orville and myself lived together, played together, worked together and, in fact, thought together."

As they worked side by side in their bicycle shop, the brothers would sometimes start whistling or humming the same tune at exactly the same moment. Their voices were so much alike, a listener in another room had a hard time telling them apart.

People often remarked that Wilbur and Orville were as inseparable as twins. They shared everything from a joint bank account to their experiments with flying machines. Neither brother smoke, drank, nor married. Lifelong bachelors, they lived with their widowed father and unmarried sister in a modest frame house in Dayton, not far from the Wright Cycle Company, where they sold, repaired, and built bicycles.

After the invention of the airplane, the public was astonished to learn that the Wright brothers had no special training in science or engineering. Though they were good students, both left high school without receiving a diploma. Neither attended college. They learned more by teaching themselves than through formal schooling.

From boyhood on, each brother had a way with tools and a knack for solving problems. Even as grown men, they never lost their enthusiasm for mechanical playthings. The Wrights' favorite niece, Ivonette, later recalled:

Wilbur and Orville on the back porch of their Dayton, Ohio, house in June, 1909.

"When we were old enough to get toys, Uncle Orv and Uncle Will had a habit of playing with them until they were broken, then repairing them so that they were better than when they were bought."

They were as close as brothers can be, yet in many ways, they were different. Wilbur was four years older, an inch and a half taller, and a pound or two leaner. With a high domed forehead and long nose, he had striking hawklike features that set him apart from his younger brother.

Orville's most prominent feature was the reddish mustache he had grown in high school. Dapper and tidy, he was by far the more clothes conscious of the two. Even in the bicycle shop he wore sleeve cuffs and a blue-and-white-striped apron to protect his clothing. "I don't believe there was ever a man who could do the work he did in all kinds of dirt, oil, and grime and come out of it looking immaculate," said Ivonette. "When the job was finished he'd come out looking like he was right out of a band box."

Wilbur wasn't that fussy. Often he had to be reminded by his sister that his suit needed pressing or that something didn't match. Once she insisted that he borrow a shirt, cuff links, and an overcoat from Orville before going off to deliver an important speech.

It was hard to rattle Wilbur. He seemed very sure of himself and didn't say much. At a Fourth of July picnic one year, he put up the swings for the children, then stood aloof from the crowd for much of the day. "The strongest impression one gets of Wilbur Wright," said a friend, "is of a man who lives largely in a world of his own."

Orville was more impulsive, "bubbling over with ideas," according to his niece. Among family and friends, he had a reputation as a tease and a practical joker. Among strangers, however, he seemed uncomfortably shy. He would clam up and fade silently into the background.

Orville's greatest pleasure was to take something apart, see how it worked, and put it back together. Wilbur was more of a visionary, fascinated by the big picture rather than its individual parts. He was the one who first dreamed of building an airplane, but it was Orville's enthusiasm that carried the brothers along.

When their father was asked which of the two contributed the most and was the leader in their partnership, he gave this answer:

"Wilbur in every respect was uncommon in his intellect and attainments—

5

was a surprise to those near him. But he seemed not to care for notice. Orville's mind grew steadily, and in invention he was fully equal to his brother. They are equal in their inventions, neither claiming any superiority above the other, nor accepting any honor to the neglect of the other."

Wilbur was born on a farm near Millville, Indiana, on April 16, 1867. Orville was born in Dayton on August 19, 1871, in the house on Hawthorn Street where the family finally settled. There were two older boys, Reuchlin and Lorin, and a younger girl, Katharine. They were the children of Bishop Milton Wright, a minister of the United Brethren Church, and his wife Susan.

The Wright family home at 7 Hawthorn Street in Dayton. Orville was born here.

Wilbur and Orville's father, Bishop Milton Wright.　　　*The brothers' mother, Susan Koerner Wright.*

Wilbur and Orville believed that their mechanical aptitude came from their mother, a shy and retiring woman who enjoyed working with her hands. Once she built a sled for her children that was passed down through the family. When the boys wanted help with a mechanical project, they went to Susan. Their father had trouble driving a nail straight.

Bishop Wright wasn't handy himself, but he recognized that talent in his younger sons, and he encouraged them. A man of iron will and absolute self-confidence, Milton believed that hard work would bring results. He taught his sons that with resolve and determination, they could accomplish anything they set out to do.

7

"We were lucky enough to grow up in an environment where there was always much encouragement to children to pursue intellectual interests, to investigate whatever aroused curiosity," Orville recalled. "In a different kind of environment, our curiosity might have been nipped long before it could have borne fruit."

Susan Wright died of tuberculosis in 1889, too soon to know what would become of her sons. Wilbur, who had stayed at home to care for his mother during her long illness, was twenty-two at the time. Orville had just left high school to start his own printing business. Katharine, not yet fifteen, replaced her mother as the woman of the family, cooking and keeping house for her father and brothers. When she left for Oberlin College in Ohio, a housekeeper took over the chores. Katharine became the family's only college graduate.

After Reuchlin and Lorin married and went out into the world, Katharine, Orville, and Wilbur continued to live with their father, forming a tight-knit family foursome. Katharine taught Latin and English at Steele High School in Dayton. She supervised the Wright household and continued to "mother" her two bachelor brothers.

The Wrights' younger sister, Katharine, at the time of her graduation from Oberlin College in 1898.

Bishop Wright lived to be eighty-eight—long enough to be taken for an airplane ride by his famous sons at a time when an airplane still seemed like a miracle.

The Wright brothers always claimed that their interest in flight began with a gift their father brought home when Wilbur was eleven and Orville seven. Bishop Wright came into the house with the surprise partly hidden in his hands. Before the boys could guess what it was, he tossed it into the air.

It was a toy helicopter made of cork, bamboo, and paper, powered by a twisted rubber band attached to twin propellers. Wilbur and Orville called it "the Bat" and played with it until it fell apart. "We built a number of copies of this toy, which flew successfully," Orville remembered. "But when we undertook to fly the toy on a much larger scale, it failed to work so well. The reason for this was not understood by us at the time, so we finally abandoned the experiments."

When Orville was eight . . .   *. . . his brother Wilbur was twelve.*

Growing up, the boys were always tinkering. Orville built kites and sold them to classmates. Wilbur, who made pocket money by helping out on a church newspaper edited by his father, constructed a special machine to fold the papers for mailing. Together, the brothers built a foot-powered wood lathe with a treadle wide enough to accommodate the feet of several neighborhood boys.

For several years, Bishop Wright's church duties kept the family on the move. Wilbur attended high school in Richmond, Indiana, but had to leave in his senior year when the Wrights moved back to Dayton. Instead of returning to school to earn his diploma, he went to work as business manager of his father's church paper.

Orville's big enthusiasm was printing. Starting with a toy press, he soon built his own press out of odd parts scrounged from a junkyard. An old tombstone served as a flat press bed for the movable type. He spent his summer vacations working as an apprentice for a Dayton printer and became an expert typesetter.

During his junior year in high school, Orville designed and built another, larger press with Wilbur's help. Also made from scrap parts, it had a frame constructed of firewood. The hinged bars of a folding buggy top maintained pressure between paper and type. While the press looked makeshift, it could print a thousand pages an hour.

Orville was so taken with printing that he dropped out of school that year to open his own printing shop. He hired a friend, Ed Sines, as his assistant. Sines recalled the day a veteran printer came by and asked to see Orville's homemade press: "He went into the press room, stood by the machine, looked at it, then sat down beside it and finally crawled underneath it. After he had been under the machine some little time he got up and said, 'Well, it works, but I certainly don't see how.'"

Bishop Wright's work in editing and publishing church newspapers inspired Orville to put out a paper of his own—a four-page neighborhood weekly called the *West Side News* (10 cents for 6 weeks, 20 cents for three months). The first issue appeared on March 1, 1889, when Orville was seventeen. He was listed on the masthead as "Publisher." Wilbur, who had always enjoyed writing, soon joined his brother as the paper's "Editor."

The brothers published the West Side News *every week for a year.*

After a year, they decided to convert their weekly into a daily, *The Evening Item.* The brothers worked hard to make the paper a success. They subscribed to a wire service, scoured the West Side for local news, and offered comment and opinion on the editorial page. But the *Item* couldn't compete with the big Dayton dailies, and after three months, it folded.

Their next venture was to set themselves up in business as Wright and Wright, Job Printers. They moved to larger quarters down the street, and with Ed Sines's help, turned out business cards, posters, advertising circulars, and announcements for local merchants and clubs.

By this time, a bicycle craze was sweeping the country. The introduction of the safety bicycle, with its two equal-sized wheels, air-filled rubber tires, a chain-driven transmission system, and other improvements, had made bicycling truly popular for the first time. Wilbur and Orville bought bikes and quickly became avid cyclists.

While Wilbur preferred long country rides, Orville went in for racing. Years later he admitted that his racing career was a disappointment. "How I used to envy you and some of the other fellows in those days," he told an old friend. When asked why the inventor of the airplane should envy a cyclist, Orville replied: "If you had eaten as much dust as I did, you'd know."

Friends began to bring their bikes around for repairs, and the brothers gained a reputation as skillful mechanics. Finally, in 1892, they put Ed Sines in charge of their printing business, formed the Wright Cycle Company, and opened a new shop across the street. As their bicycle business grew, they moved to larger quarters, opening a series of four shops in succession.

The Wright brothers' bicycle shop at 1127 West Third Street in Dayton.

12

At first they simply sold, rented, and repaired bicycles. Then they began to manufacture them, turning out two custom-built models, the Van Cleve and the less-expensive St. Clair. The brothers made many of the parts themselves, using simple tools like a turret lathe, a drill press, and tube-cutting equipment. They even built a one-cylinder internal-combustion engine to drive the machinery in their workshop.

When the bicycling season ended each year, Wilbur and Orville had plenty of spare time. They added front and side porches to the family house, installed shutters on all the windows, and built a fireplace in the parlor. Recently they had become camera bugs, so they converted a shed behind the house into a photographic darkroom, where they developed glass-plate negatives and made their own prints.

Then they discovered a new interest. By 1899 they were working enthusiastically in the back room of the bike shop on the idea of a lifetime.

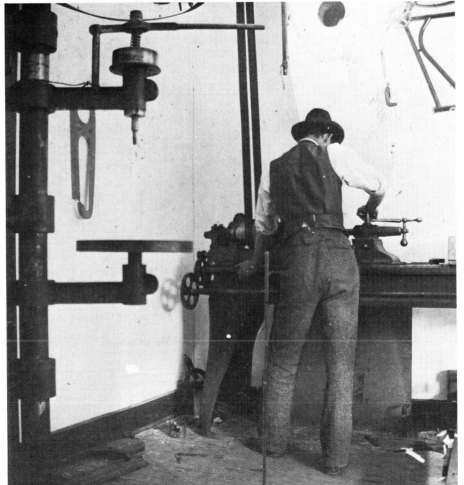

Wilbur in the bicycle shop workroom, 1897.

13

Otto Lilienthal gliding.

THREE

The Art of Flying

While the Wright brothers were building bicycles in Dayton, an engineer named Otto Lilienthal was conducting gliding experiments from the top of a small hill in Germany. Lilienthal had become famous for his pioneering flights with hang gliders. He would strap a glider to his back and run quickly down a hill until the glider's wings were lifted by the wind.

Stories about the red-bearded, barrel-chested "Flying Man" appeared in newspapers and magazines the world over. Photographs showed him soaring through the air on batlike wings. He was at the height of his fame when one of his gliders stalled during a Sunday afternoon flight on August 9, 1896. It plunged 50 feet, breaking Lilienthal's spine. He died the next day in a Berlin hospital. His last words: "Sacrifices must be made."

Lilienthal wasn't the first to sacrifice his life in an effort to fly. Since the earliest times, earthbound humans had envied the freedom of birds and dreamed of imitating them. An ancient Greek myth tells the story of Daedalus and his son Icarus, who escaped from a prison on the island of Crete by making wings out of feathers and wax. Together they flew away, but Icarus became too confident. He flew so high that the heat of the sun melted the wax in his wings, and he fell into the sea and drowned.

Down through the centuries, many a would-be birdman met ridicule or death. At Wiltshire Abbey in England during the eleventh century, a brave but foolhardy Benedictine monk named Eilmer was convinced that he could fly. He made wings for himself by stretching linen over a wooden frame, then gluing duck and chicken feathers to the cloth. He climbed to the top of the abbey tower, tied the wings to his arms and legs, and prepared for takeoff.

"Collecting the breeze on the summit of the tower, he flew for more than the distance of a furlong [about an eighth of a mile]," reported a fellow monk, the British historian William of Malmesbury. "But, agitated by the violence of the wind and the swirling of air, as well as by awareness of his rashness, he fell, broke his legs, and was lame ever after. He himself used to say that the cause of his failure was his forgetting to put a tail on the back part."

The Aerial Steam Carriage, *designed by William Henson and John Stringfield in 1842. Though this aircraft was never built, its forward-looking appearance influenced many future experimenters.*

In Italy during the early 1500s, the great artist and scientist Leonardo da Vinci gave serious thought to flying. He analyzed the flight of birds and drew detailed sketches of several heavier-than-air flying machines, including a muscle-powered helicopter. But he did not publish his ideas, and a practical airplane remained nothing but a dream.

After Leonardo, hopeful inventors suggested flying machines that would navigate the ocean of air by means of sails or oars, by flapping wings, or by paddle wheels. The first person to envision the airplane in its present-day form was Sir George Cayley, a British baronet who made a systematic study of bird flight and aeronautics during the early 1800s. He conceived of the airplane as a machine with fixed wings, a fuselage, and a tail, and with separate systems to provide lift, propulsion, and control.

Cayley built and flew the world's first successful model glider in 1804. Later he built two full-size gliders capable of brief flights with a pilot aboard. One of these machines carried his reluctant coachman on a gliding flight in 1853. After a bumpy landing, the coachman told his employer: "Please, Sir George, I wish to give notice. I was hired to drive, and not to fly." While Cayley never achieved his goal of powered flight, or lived to see the Wright brothers do it, he was the first to grasp and describe the essential principles of flight.

By the late 1800s, a few dedicated scientists and engineers were beginning to make real progress in their study of aeronautics. One group of experimenters worked with small model airplanes, powered by miniature steam engines, by clockwork mechanisms, or by twisted rubber strands. If a powered model could be made to fly, they reasoned, then it would be possible to "scale up" the model and build a full-size, passenger-carrying airplane.

Other researchers were convinced that the conquest of the air would begin not with models, but with man-carrying gliders. Only by testing unpowered gliders in actual flight, they believed, could an inventor gain a feel for handling a craft in the air. With enough gliding experience, he would be able to design a powered machine capable of sustaining flight with a pilot aboard.

Otto Lilienthal was the most influential of these gliding pioneers. "One can get a proper insight into the practice of flying only by actual flying experiments," he said. During the early 1890s he built sixteen distinct versions of his basic hang glider, including monoplanes (one pair of wings) and biplanes (two pair.) The muslin-covered wings were curved from root to tip and could

Otto Lilienthal built sixteen different versions of his basic hang glider . . .

. . . and tried to keep the gliders balanced by shifting his weight.

be folded back like the wings of a bat. Once aloft, Lilienthal tried to keep his gliders balanced by shifting his weight from side to side as he hung suspended by his armpits beneath the giant wings.

He made close to two thousand gliding flights before falling to his death. His experiments helped convince many skeptics that a human could fly, and he inspired the Wright brothers, among others, to try their own luck at gliding.

The best-known experimenter with model airplanes was an American. Dr. Samuel Pierpont Langley, a distinguished scientist, was head of the Smithsonian Institution in Washington, D.C. Langley spent ten years testing models on an indoor track before settling on his basic design—two pair of curved wings, one pair behind the other, with a little steam engine and twin propellers in between. He called the models *aerodromes,* from the Greek words meaning "air runner."

Finally ready for outdoor trials, Langley prepared to launch his models from a catapult mounted atop a houseboat in the Potomac River, not far from Washington. Success came on May 6, 1896, when a 26-pound aerodrome, with a wingspan of 14 feet, shot out over the river and stayed aloft for 90 seconds. With its brass fittings glistening in the sunlight, the miniature airplane flew for half a mile at a speed of 20 to 25 miles an hour and came down only when the steam in its boiler was exhausted. Six months later, a larger model flew for three-quarters of a mile.

Impressed with these flights, the U.S. Army gave Langley $50,000 to continue his experiments, and the Smithsonian threw in $20,000 more—a sizable fortune in those days. If anyone could build a full-size, passenger-carrying, powered flying machine, it seemed, it would be Samuel Pierpont Langley.

Another American working on the problem of flight was Octave Chanute, a civil engineer with a white goatee. He was famous for building the first bridge across the wide Missouri in 1868. Chanute had visited Otto Lilienthal in Germany and returned home determined to conduct his own gliding experiments. The gliders he designed had wings mounted on rubber springs, so they could rock back and forth when struck by wind gusts. Between 1896 and 1898, Chanute and his assistants made hundreds of flight tests on the windswept sand dunes at the foot of Lake Michigan. They stayed aloft as long as 14 seconds—within 1 second of the longest glide ever made by Lilienthal.

Octave Chanute, gliding pioneer and friend of the Wrights.

Chanute's assistants testing one of his gliders over the sand dunes near Lake Michigan, 1896.

In Washington, meanwhile, Dr. Langley was building a full-size, gasoline-powered airplane patterned on his successful flying models. Called the *Great Aerodrome*, it was 55 feet long, with a wingspan of 48 feet. Like the models that inspired it, the *Great Aerodrome* would be catapulted into the air from the roof of a houseboat anchored in the Potomac.

The first trial took place on October 7, 1903. That morning, a brave young engineer named Charles Manly, wearing a cork-lined life jacket and automobile goggles, climbed into the fabric-sided pilot's car suspended beneath the airplane. He stood upright before the controls, revved up the engine, then gave the signal to release the spring-loaded catapult. A rocket was fired to alert the newspaper photographers waiting on shore. The machine lunged forward, zoomed off its launching track, and—as one reporter wrote—"simply slid into the water like a handful of mortar." Drenched but unhurt, Manly was rescued, while the *Aerodrome* was fished out of the Potomac.

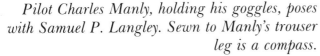

Pilot Charles Manly, holding his goggles, poses with Samuel P. Langley. Sewn to Manly's trouser leg is a compass.

Langley's 55-foot-long, man-carrying Great Aerodrome, *October, 1903. Launched from the roof of a houseboat . . .*

A second trial took place on December 8. Manly had agreed to risk his life again. Again, the *Great Aerodrome* slid into the icy river. As Manly was hauled to safety, a doctor standing by had to cut the frozen clothing from his shivering body.

Langley blamed the catapult for catching part of the machine as it tried to take off. His critics said that the design of the *Aerodrome* was at fault, that it was never capable of flight. In any case, the army refused to advance more money, and Langley's expensive project ended in failure.

Newspapers around the country had a field day poking fun at Langley and his soggy *Aerodrome*. The *Boston Herald* suggested that the scientist should concentrate his efforts on submarines rather than flying machines. *The New York Times* commented that a man-carrying airplane would eventually be built—but only if mathematicians and engineers worked steadily for the next one million to ten million years.

It didn't take that long at all. Exactly nine days after Langley's *Great Aerodrome* sank into the Potomac, Orville Wright took off on history's first successful airplane flight.

23

. . . and fell into the river.

the airplane collapsed upon itself immediately after takeoff

The Wright brothers' windblown camp near Kitty Hawk, North Carolina, in 1900.

FOUR

Wind and Sand

Otto Lilienthal's gliding experiments in Germany, and his dramatic death in 1896, had aroused the Wright brothers' curiosity. They began to read what little they could find published on the subject of flight.

"We knew that men had by common consent adopted human flight as the standard of impossibility," wrote Wilbur. "When a man said, 'It can't be done, a man might as well learn to fly,' he was understood as expressing the final limit of impossibility.

"Our own growing belief that man might nevertheless learn to fly was based on the idea that while thousands of the most dissimilar body structures, such as insects, reptiles, birds and mammals were flying every day at pleasure, it was reasonable to suppose that man might also fly."

In the spring of 1899, Wilbur wrote to the Smithsonian Institution and asked for information about flight experiments. "I wish to avail myself of all that is already known," he said. The Smithsonian replied by sending a selection of pamphlets and a list of available books, including Samuel Pierpont Langley's *Experiments in Aerodynamics* and Octave Chanute's *Progress in Flying Machines*. The Wrights later sought advice from both men. Chanute took a fatherly interest in helping them and became an enthusiastic friend and supporter.

As the brothers studied the infant science of aeronautics, they found that a practical heavier-than-air flying machine would have to meet three basic requirements. It would need wings that could lift it into the air, a power plant to propel it through the air, and a means of controlling the machine in flight.

The first two problems had been solved to some extent. Experimenters already knew that an aircraft's wings should be curved—convex on top and concave beneath. When such a wing slices through the air, its shape produces reduced air pressure above the wing and increased pressure below. The resulting upward push, called *lift*, is what raises a plane or a bird off the ground.

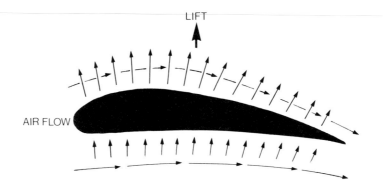

LIFT: Air streaming across the upper and lower surfaces of a curved wing, or airfoil, *will keep it aloft. Early experimenters tried to design a wing that would take the greatest advantage of this fact.*

Gliding pioneers like Lilienthal and Chanute had actually designed and built wings that would lift a person into the air. In fact, they had worked out the simple equations and engineering data that would enable others to design wings.

As for a power plant, Samuel Langley's steam-driven model aerodromes had shown that it was possible to build an engine-propeller combination that would propel a set of wings through the air.

The problem of control, however, was far from being solved. Once aloft, an aviator would have to steer his craft and keep it on an even keel. Experimenters still tended to think of a flying machine as a ship of the air. It seemed obvious that a rudder at the rear of the machine would work the same way as a ship's rudder, swinging the craft's tail around and steering it to the right or left.

From there it was a short step to the idea of a horizontal rudder, or *elevator,* which would permit an aviator to turn the nose of his craft up or down, in order to climb or descend. Elevators were already being used for that purpose in submarines. Of course, no one knew for sure if rudders and elevators would work in the air as they did at sea, since no one had ever piloted a powered aircraft.

Besides steering to the right or left, and turning its nose up or down, a flying machine was subject to a third kind of motion. It could roll from side to side, dipping one wing and then the other. Everyone realized that there had to be some way of controlling this side-to-side rocking motion. Unless its wings could be balanced, an aircraft might roll out of control as it navigated the turbulent sea of air.

The Wrights were surprised that the problem of balance and control had received so little attention. Lilienthal had attempted to balance his gliders by resorting to acrobatic body movements, swinging his torso and thrashing his legs. Langley's model aerodromes were capable of simple straight-line flights but could not be steered or maneuvered. His goal was to get a man into the air first and work out a control system later.

Wilbur and Orville had other ideas. It seemed to them that an effective means of controlling an aircraft was the key to successful flight. What was needed was a control system that an airborne pilot could operate, a system that would keep a flying machine balanced and on course as it climbed and descended, or as it turned and circled in the air. Like bicycling, flying required balance in motion.

A few weeks after writing to the Smithsonian, the Wright brothers made their first important discovery. As they watched buzzards gliding and soaring in the skies over Dayton, they noticed that the birds kept adjusting the positions of their outstretched wings. First one wing was high, then the other.

It occurred to the brothers that a bird can balance itself and control its flight by changing the angle at which each wing meets the oncoming air. When the bird wants to begin a turn, for example, it tilts the leading edge of one wing up to generate more lift, making that wing rise. At the same time, it tilts the leading edge of the opposite wing down, causing that wing to drop. Its body revolves toward the lowered wing. When it has revolved as far as it wishes, it reverses the process and begins to roll the other way.

29

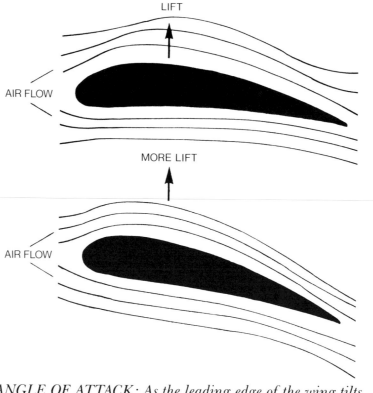

LIFT

AIR FLOW

MORE LIFT

AIR FLOW

ANGLE OF ATTACK: As the leading edge of the wing tilts upward, air moves faster over the top of the wing, increasing its lift and making the wing rise. When the leading edge of the wing tilts downward, the wing loses lift and drops. The angle at which the wing meets the oncoming air is called the angle of attack.

By tilting its right and left wings at opposite angles—one wing up, the other down—the bird can lean to one side or the other. It can make graceful banking turns and then level off. And it can correct the rocking motion of its wings.

"We could not understand that there was anything about a bird that could not be built on a larger scale and used by man," Orville wrote later. If a bird adjusts the angles of its wings to make turns or to balance itself, why not apply the same idea to an aircraft's wings?

And yet an aircraft's wings were rigid. How could they be tilted or twisted like the wings of a bird? The answer came to Wilbur one day in the bicycle shop, after he had taken an inner tube out of its long cardboard box. As he stood chatting with his customer, he idly twisted the ends of the box in opposite directions. Looking down at his hands, he saw the solution: a spiral twist running along an aircraft's wings would make it possible to tilt one wing up and the other down.

To test Wilbur's idea, the Wrights designed their first experimental aircraft. In the workroom of the bicycle shop, they built a biplane glider with a five-foot wingspan, designed to be flown as a kite. The kite's controls could be worked from the ground by means of cords running from the wingtips to sticks held upright in either hand. By tilting the sticks, the kite flier could twist the right and left wingtips in opposite directions, and could also raise or lower the flat tail attached to the wings.

Wilbur took the kite out to a field where he and Orville had flown kites as boys. He sent it spiraling into the air. The sight of a grown man flying a double-decker kite almost as wide as he was tall attracted a troop of neighborhood boys. They stood watching as Wilbur worked the controls. The kite responded instantly. It climbed, dived, and rolled to the right or left on command. Once, when Wilbur shifted the wings, the kite swooped down so steeply that the boys threw themselves on the ground to avoid getting hit.

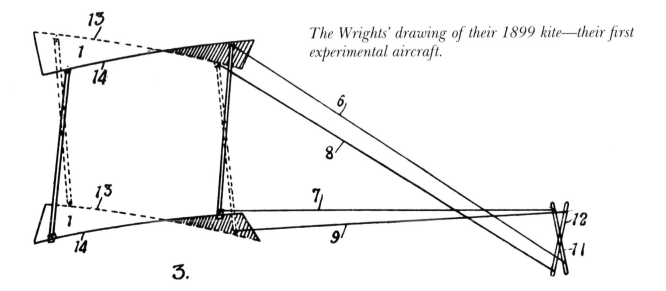

The Wrights' drawing of their 1899 kite—their first experimental aircraft.

This one test convinced the brothers that they were on the right track. The next step was to test their control system on a full-size, man-carrying glider. For that, they would need a suitable testing ground, a place with strong steady winds and plenty of open space. Wilbur wrote to the U.S. Weather Bureau in Washington and was sent a list of the windiest Weather Bureau stations in the country.

One site sounded ideal, though they had never heard of it before—a remote fishing village called Kitty Hawk, on the Outer Banks of North Carolina. The winds in Kitty Hawk averaged 10 to 20 miles an hour. The Outer Banks offered endless stretches of sandy beach, perfect for soft landings, and plenty of solitude, so the brothers could experiment in secret. They decided to take a vacation from their bicycle shop when the busy season ended the following year. They would test a new and bigger glider at Kitty Hawk.

Wilbur planned to go on ahead and make arrangements. Shortly before leaving he wrote to his father, who was away on church business, that he would be conducting some experiments with a flying machine: "It is my belief that flight is possible and while I am taking up the investigation for pleasure rather than profit, I think there is a slight possibility of achieving fame and fortune from it. . . . At any rate I shall have an outing of several weeks and see a part of the world I have never before visited."

And so Wilbur set off on the great adventure of his life, heading for the most isolated spot on the Eastern Seaboard. He traveled by train and ferry to Norfolk, Virginia, then by train again to Elizabeth City, North Carolina. In those days, there were no bridges connecting the Outer Banks to the North Carolina mainland. Wilbur planned to hire a boat for the overwater trip to Kitty Hawk, but he was surprised to find that "no one seemed to know anything about the place, or how to get there."

After scouring the Elizabeth City waterfront for three days, he finally met Israel Perry, an old salt who had grown up in Kitty Hawk. Perry offered to take Wilbur and his baggage to the Outer Banks on his flat-bottomed fishing schooner, the *Curlicue*. As Wilbur boarded the boat, "I discovered at a glance that . . . The sails were rotten, the ropes badly worn and the rudderpost half rotted off, and the cabin so dirty and vermin-infested that I kept out of it from first to last."

Kitty Hawk was only about 35 miles across Albemarle Sound, but it took two days to get there. First the *Curlicue* sprang a leak, and all hands had to pitch in and start bailing. Then they had to sit out a raging storm as the boat rolled wildly and waves crashed over the stern, drenching everyone. "Israel had for so long been a stranger to the touch of water upon his skin that it affects him very much," Wilbur wrote in his journal. Finally the storm passed and the rusty old scow sailed grandly into Kitty Hawk Bay.

The village was a lonely settlement of a few weather-beaten houses scattered among the trees that lined the bay. About a mile to the east, directly on the ocean, stood a station of the U.S. Lifesaving Service. In between there was nothing but sand.

Wilbur reached Kitty Hawk on September 13, 1900. Orville joined him a week and a half later, after crossing Albemarle Sound in a sailboat. They stayed with the family of William Tate, the local postmaster, until they could set up their own camp about a half-mile away.

After that, Wilbur and Orville lived in a tent. They had brought along three trunkloads of camping equipment—folding canvas cots, an acetylene lamp, canned and packaged food supplies. Orville had his mandolin, Wilbur

Kitty Hawk postmaster William Tate with his family. The Wrights stayed with the Tates until they could set up their own camp in 1900.

Wilbur scouring pots and pans in the sand outside the brothers' tent.

34

his harmonica. Orville did the cooking, Wilbur the dishwashing. They had to carry their water in buckets a thousand feet over the sand to their tent. When they looked out the tent door, they saw eagles soaring overhead and buzzards by the dozen. In the evening, fish hawks and cranes flapped softly across the salt marshes.

However, the surroundings weren't always so idyllic, especially in the middle of the night when sudden squalls threatened to blow their tent away. "The wind shaking the roof and sides of the tent sounds exactly like thunder," Orville wrote to his sister. "When we crawl out of the tent to fix things outside, the sand fairly blinds us. It blows across the ground in clouds. We certainly can't complain of the place. We came down here for wind and sand, and we have got them."

Like the proper young gentlemen they were, Wilbur and Orville faced the sand and grit of each new day wearing neckties and high stiff collars. Not many outsiders visited Kitty Hawk. The locals were fascinated by the two brothers from Dayton and their odd ways. "Every place we go we are called Mr. Wright," Orville reported. "Our fame has spread far and wide up and down the beach."

Their new glider had been crated and shipped in parts by train and boat for assembly at Kitty Hawk. A biplane with a 17-foot wingspan, it had a lightweight wooden frame covered with tightly-woven cotton sateen. The total cost of the materials had come to $15.

This was not a hang glider like those built by Lilienthal and Chanute, where the pilot hung suspended beneath the machine. Instead, the pilot would lie facedown on the lower wing, his hands gripping the forward rudder, or elevator, and his feet planted firmly in a pivoted T-bar. By tilting the elevator up or down, he could make the glider nose up or nose down. The T-bar was connected by wires and pulleys to the wings. By pushing on the bar with his right or left foot, the pilot could twist the wings at opposite angles. When the right wing was twisted up, the left wing was automatically twisted down. Hopefully, this *wing warping*, as the brothers called it, would keep the glider balanced as it flew.

"It is not to have a motor and is not expected to fly in any true sense," Wilbur reassured his father. "My idea is merely to experiment and practice with a view of solving the problem of equilibrium. . . . In my experiments I do

36

not expect to rise many feet from the ground, and in case I am upset there is nothing but soft sand to strike on. I do not intend to take dangerous chances, both because I have no wish to get hurt and because a fall would stop my experimenting, which I would not like at all."

On windy autumn days they flew their glider. To start with they tested it as an unmanned kite, with lines running to the ground to operate the controls.

The 1900 Wright glider being flown as an unmanned kite at Kitty Hawk.

After three weeks of tests, measurements, adjustments, and repairs, they were ready to attempt free flights with a pilot aboard. Bill Tate, the postmaster, arranged for a horse and wagon to haul the 50-pound glider nearly 4 miles down the beach to a cluster of giant sand dunes called Kill Devil Hills. When the three men arrived at the site, they unloaded the glider and carried it nearly a hundred feet up the side of Big Hill, the tallest dune. The slope of Big Hill would serve as their launching platform.

Wilbur was the pilot. When he was in position on the lower wing and ready to start, Orville and Bill Tate each grabbed a wingtip and ran forward into the wind. As the breeze flowed over the wings, the glider seemed to stir to life. It became lighter in the handlers' grasp and began to fly on its own. As it lifted itself, Wilbur shouted "Let go!" For a few thrilling moments he lay motionless between the great white wings, sailing down the slope, picking up speed as he rode sea-scented breezes above the dunes. Never before, except in stories or dreams, had a man lying prone like a bird been carried through the air by a pair of wings.

That day Wilbur made about a dozen flights. His best glides lasted between 15 and 20 seconds and covered 300 to 400 feet. As it turned out, those were the only free glides of the year. Afterward the winds weren't strong enough to let them glide again.

Altogether, Wilbur spent a grand total of perhaps 2 minutes in the air—not much, but long enough to show that their control system was working. They would need a lot more practice before they could operate the controls smoothly and make longer flights. But there was reason for hope, and even enthusiasm. As Wilbur put it: "We were very much pleased with the general results of the trip, for setting out as we did, with almost revolutionary theories on many points, and an entirely untried form of machine, we considered it quite a point to be able to return without having our pet theories completely knocked in the head . . . and our own brains dashed out in the bargain."

They were already planning to build a bigger and better glider and return to Kitty Hawk the following summer. Before packing up and leaving, they told Bill Tate that he could salvage the old glider if he wanted to go to the trouble of hauling it all the way back to Kitty Hawk. He did, dismantling the machine in his front yard. Mrs. Tate used the white sateen wing covering to make dresses for their two little girls, Irene and Pauline.

The 1900 glider wrecked by the wind.

In Dayton that winter, Wilbur and Orville designed and built a new glider. With wings 22 feet across and 7 feet deep, it would be the biggest glider ever flown. It weighed nearly 100 pounds. For protection during landings, it was equipped with skids like sled runners.

Instead of a foot control, the wing-warping wires were now connected to a wooden hip cradle on the lower wing. As the pilot took his place, his hips slid into the cradle. By shifting his hips to one side or the other, he could twist one wing up and the other down to keep the glider on an even keel. If the left wing dropped, for example, he would shift his hips to the right, restoring balance. His hands were free to operate the forward rudder, or elevator.

The brothers returned to Kitty Hawk on July 10, 1901. This year they wanted to be closer to their launching site at Kill Devil Hills, so they loaded their camping equipment, glider parts, and some lumber into a beach cart, drove it 4 miles south, and set up camp a few hundred feet from the bottom of Big Hill. Again they lived in a tent, but they also put up a large wooden shed to use as a workshop and hangar for the new glider. This year they would share their camp with visitors. Their friend Octave Chanute and two associates joined the Wrights for a few days to observe their experiments and to test a new glider that Chanute had recently designed.

They had scarcely settled in when torrential rains swept over the Outer Banks, lasting a solid week without letup, followed by the worst outbreak of mosquitoes in years. "There was no escape," Orville reported to Katharine. "The sand and grass and trees and hills and everything was fairly covered with them. They chewed us clear through our underwear and socks. Lumps began swelling up all over my body like hen's eggs."

The mosquitoes finally disappeared, but the brothers' troubles were just beginning. When they assembled their glider and began to test it, they were sadly disappointed. "The machine refused to act like our machine last year and at times seemed to be entirely beyond control," wrote Orville.

Orville poses beside the upended 1901 glider—the biggest glider ever flown up to that time.

Octave Chanute and friends visited the Wrights' Kill Devil Hills camp in 1901. The ends of the wooden shed opened upward, providing easy removal of the glider and welcome shade from the summer sun. The brothers' tent and water pump can be seen to the left.

Once again, Wilbur acted as pilot. Some of his glides were as good or better than the year before, and yet one problem after another cropped up. They had designed the glider's wings according to air-pressure tables published by Otto Lilienthal, but the wings didn't have nearly the lifting power the Wrights had expected. To make matters worse, the forward elevator, controlling up-and-down movements, wasn't as effective as they had hoped.

Launching the 1901 glider. Wilbur is at the controls, while Bill Tate and his brother Dan assist at the wingtips.

The Wrights stopped testing and spent a week altering the shape of the wings, tinkering with the elevator, and making other adjustments. This improved the action of the elevator, but the glider still failed to lift and perform as Lilienthal's tables had predicted. Then the brothers encountered a mysterious problem with the wing-warping system. At times when the wings were being warped, the glider showed an alarming tendency to spin out of control.

One day as Wilbur was skimming over the sand, the left wing dipped. He shifted his hips to the right, but instead of leveling off, the glider spun around and crashed into the sand, throwing him forward onto the elevator. The front of the machine was badly damaged, and Wilbur suffered facial cuts, a bruised nose, and a black eye.

After that the brothers flew the glider as an unmanned kite, operating the wing-warping control from the ground. The machine continued to spin out of control. They could not figure out what went wrong.

Then the rains returned, dampening their spirits even more. There seemed no point in continuing their tests. Instead of improving on their first glider, they had created a whole new set of problems. Puzzled and dejected, they closed their camp at the end of August, sooner than they had planned, and went back to Dayton.

"We doubted that we would ever resume our experiments," Wilbur wrote later. "When we looked at the time and money which we had expended, and considered the progress made and the distance yet to go, we considered our experiments a failure. At this time I made the prediction that man would sometime fly, but that it would not be in our lifetime."

Wilbur in flight.

FIVE

Back to the Drawing Board

The experiments that Wilbur and Orville had carried out with their latest glider in 1901 were far from encouraging. Reflecting on their problems, Wilbur observed: "We saw that the calculations upon which all flying machines had been based were unreliable, and that all were simply groping in the dark. Having set out with absolute faith in the existing scientific data, we were driven to doubt one thing after another, till finally, after two years of experiment, we cast it all aside, and decided to rely entirely on our own investigations."

In the gaslit workroom behind their bicycle shop, Wilbur and Orville began to compile their own data. They wanted to test different types of wing surfaces and obtain accurate air-pressure tables. To do this, they built a wind tunnel—a wooden box 6 feet long with a glass viewing window on top and a fan at one end. It wasn't the world's first wind tunnel, but it would be the first to yield valuable results for the construction of a practical airplane.

The materials needed to make model wings, or *airfoils,* and the tools to shape them were right at hand. Using tin shears, hammers, files, and a soldering iron, the brothers fashioned as many as two hundred miniature wings out of tin, galvanized iron, steel, solder, and wax. They made wings that were thick or thin, curved or flat, wings with rounded tips and pointed tips, slender wings and stubby wings. They attached these experimental airfoils to balances made of bicycle spokes and old hacksaw blades. Then they tested the wings in their wind tunnel to see how they behaved in a moving airstream.

Wilbur and Dan Tate launch the 1902 glider with Orville at the controls.

For several weeks they were absorbed in painstaking and systematic lab work—testing, measuring, and calculating as they tried to unlock the secrets of an aircraft wing. The work was tedious. It was repetitious. Yet they would look back on that winter as a time of great excitement, when each new day promised discoveries waiting to be made. "Wilbur and I could hardly wait for morning to come," Orville declared, "to get at something that interested us. *That's* happiness."

The Wrights knew that they were exploring uncharted territory with their wind-tunnel tests. Each new bit of data jotted down in their notebooks added to their understanding of how an airfoil works. Gradually they replaced the calculations of others with facts and figures of their own. Their doubts vanished, and their faith in themselves grew. When their lab tests were finally completed, they felt confident that they could calculate in advance the performance of an aircraft's wings with far greater accuracy than had ever before been possible.

A replica of the Wrights' pioneering wind tunnel.

48

Using this cleverly designed device inside their wind tunnel, the Wrights were able to test the lift and drag of their experimental airfoils.

Armed with this new knowledge, they designed their biggest glider yet. Its wings, longer and narrower than before, measured 32 feet from tip to tip and 5 feet from front to rear. For the first time, the new glider had a tail—two 6-foot-high vertical fins, designed to help stabilize the machine during turns. The hip cradle developed the year before to control wing warping was retained. The craft weighed just under 120 pounds.

With growing anticipation, Wilbur and Orville prepared for their 1902 trip to the Outer Banks. "They really ought to get away for a while," Katharine wrote to her father. "Will is thin and nervous and so is Orv. They will be all right when they get down in the sand where the salt breezes blow. . . . They think that life at Kitty Hawk cures all ills, you know.

"The flying machine is in process of making now. Will spins the sewing machine around by the hour while Orv squats around marking the places to

49

sew [the cotton wing covering]. There is no place in the house to live but I'll be lonesome enough by this time next week and wish I could have some of their racket around."

The brothers reached the Outer Banks at the end of August with their trunks, baggage, and crates carrying the glider parts. At Kill Devil Hills, they found that their wooden shed from the year before had been battered by winter storms. They set to work making repairs and remodeling the building, so they could use it instead of a tent as their new living quarters.

"We fitted up our living arrangements much more comfortably than last year," Wilbur reported. "Our kitchen is immensely improved, and then we have made beds on the second floor and now sleep aloft. It is an improvement over cots. We also have a bicycle which runs much better over the sand than we hoped, so that it takes only about an hour to make the round trip to Kitty Hawk instead of three hours as before. There are other improvements . . . so we are having a splendid time."

"Our kitchen is immensely improved . . .

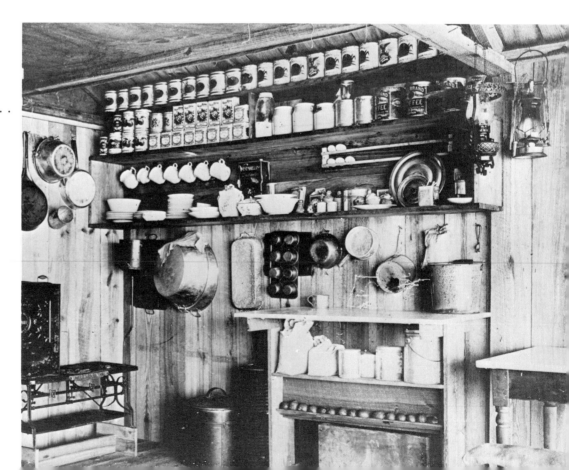

. . . and we have made beds on the second floor and now sleep aloft."

By the middle of September they had assembled their new glider and were ready to try it out. This year they took turns in the pilot's position, giving Orville a chance to fly for the first time. To begin with, they were very cautious. They would launch the machine from the slope on Big Hill and glide only a short distance as they practiced working the controls. Steering to the right or left was accomplished by warping the wings, with the glider always turning toward the lower wing. Up-and-down movements were controlled by the forward elevator.

In a few days they made dozens of short but successful test glides. At this point, things looked more promising than ever. The only mishap occurred one afternoon when Orville was at the controls. That evening he recorded the incident in his diary:

"I was sailing along smoothly without any trouble . . . when I noticed that one wing was getting a little too high and that the machine was slowly sliding off in the opposite direction. . . . The next thing I knew was that the wing was very high in the air, a great deal higher than before, and I thought I must have worked the twisting apparatus the wrong way. Thinking of nothing else . . . I threw the wingtips to their greatest angle. By this time I found suddenly

51

Flying the 1902 glider as a kite.

that I was making a descent backwards toward the low wing, from a height of 25 or 30 feet. . . . The result was a heap of flying machine, cloth and sticks in a heap, with me in the center without a bruise or scratch. The experiments thereupon suddenly came to a close till repairs can be made. In spite of this sad catastrophe we are tonight in a hilarious mood as a result of the encouraging performance of the machine."

A few days' labor made the glider as good as new. It wasn't seriously damaged again during hundreds of test glides, and it repeatedly withstood rough landings at full speed. Wilbur and Orville became more and more confident. "Our new machine is a very great improvement over anything we had built before and over anything anyone has built," Wilbur told his father. "Everything is so much more satisfactory that we now believe that the flying problem is really nearing its solution."

And yet the solution was not yet quite at hand. As they continued their test flights, a baffling new problem arose. On most flights, the glider performed almost perfectly. But every so often—in about one flight out of fifty—it would spin out of control as the pilot tried to level off after a turn.

"We were at a loss to know what the cause might be," wrote Wilbur. "The new machine . . . had a vertical tail while the earlier ones were tailless; and the wing tips were on a line with the center while the old machines had the tips drawn down like a gull's wings. The trouble might be due to either of these differences."

First they altered the wingtips and went back to Big Hill for more test flights. Again, the glider spun out of control during a turn. Then they focused their attention to the machine's 6-foot-high double-vaned tail, which was fixed rigidly in place. They had installed this tail to help stabilize the glider during turns, but now, it seemed, something was wrong.

Lying in bed one sleepless night, Orville figured out what the problem was. The fixed tail worked perfectly well most of the time. During some turns, however—when the airspeed was low and the pilot failed to level off soon enough—pressure was built up on the tail, throwing the glider off balance and into a spin. That's just what happened to Orville the day of his accident. The cure was to make the tail movable—like a ship's rudder or a bird's tail.

The next morning at breakfast, Orville told Wilbur about his idea. After thinking it over for a few minutes, Wilbur agreed. Then he offered an idea of his own. Why not connect the new movable tail to the wing-warping wires? This would allow the pilot to twist the wings and turn the tail at the same time, simply by shifting his hips. With the wings and tail coordinated, the glider would always make a smooth banked turn.

They removed the original tail and installed a movable single-vaned tail 5 feet high. From then on, there were no more problems. The movable tail rudder finally gave the Wright brothers complete control of their glider. "With this improvement our serious troubles ended," wrote Wilbur, "and thereafter we devoted ourselves to the work of gaining skill by continued practice."

As the brothers worked on their glider, their camp was filling up with visitors again. Their older brother Lorin arrived at the end of September to see what Wilbur and Orville were up to. Then Octave Chanute showed up again, along with two other gliding enthusiasts. Now six bunks were jammed into the narrow sleeping quarters up in the rafters. At night, the sounds of Wilbur's harmonica, Orville's mandolin, and a chorus of male voices drifted across the lonely dunes.

Lorin Wright took this photo of his brothers and their visitors at Kill Devil Hills in October, 1902. From left: Octave Chanute, Orville, Wilbur, Augustus M. Herring, George A. Spratt, Dan Tate.

Closeup of the modified 1902 glider in free flight.

"When the wind rose to 20 miles an hour, gliding was a real sport . . ."

Wilbur making a right turn in the 1902 glider. ▶

With their movable tail rudder, the Wrights felt confident that their glider could master the winds. They practiced flying at every opportunity, staying on at their camp until late in October, long after all their visitors had left. "Glides were made whenever weather conditions were favorable," Wilbur recalled. "Many days were lost on account of rain. Still more were lost on account of light winds. Whenever the breeze fell below six miles an hour, very hard running was required to get the machine started, and the task of carrying it back up the hill was real labor . . . but when the wind rose to 20 miles an hour, gliding was a real sport, for starting was easy and the labor of carrying the machine back uphill was performed by the wind."

One day they had a wind of about 30 miles an hour and were able to glide in it without any trouble. "That was the highest wind a gliding machine was ever in, so that we now hold all the records!" Orville wrote home. "The largest machine ever handled . . . the longest distance glide (American), the longest time in the air, the smallest angle of descent, and the highest wind!!! Well, I'll leave the rest of the 'blow' till we get home."

That season the Wrights had designed, built, and flown the world's first fully controllable aircraft. The three-dimensional system of aircraft control worked out by the brothers is the basic system used even today in all winged vehicles that depend on the atmosphere for support.

Except for an engine, their 1902 glider flew just as a Boeing 747 airliner or a jet fighter flies. A modern plane "warps" its wings in order to turn or level off by moving the ailerons on the rear edges of the wings (see drawing on page 67). It makes smooth banking turns with the aid of a movable vertical rudder. And it noses up or down by means of an elevator (usually located at the rear of the plane).

Wilbur and Orville made hundreds of perfectly controlled glides in 1902. They proved that their laboratory tests were accurate. The next step was to build a powered airplane. "Before leaving camp," Orville wrote, "we were already at work on the general design of a new machine which we proposed to propel with a motor."

SIX

Horsepower and Propellers

The Wright brothers could not just take a motor and put it into one of their gliders. First they needed a motor that was light yet powerful. Then they had to design propellers that would produce enough thrust to drive a flying machine through the air. Finally they had to build an aircraft body sturdy enough to carry the weight and withstand the vibrations of the motor and propellers.

Wilbur wrote to several manufacturers of gasoline engines, asking if they could supply an engine that would produce at least 8 horsepower, yet weigh less than 200 pounds. No company was willing to take on the assignment. Wilbur and Orville decided to build the motor themselves with the help of Charlie Taylor, a mechanic they had hired to help out in the bicycle shop.

"We didn't make any drawings," Taylor later recalled. "One of us would sketch out the part we were talking about on a piece of scratch paper and I'd spike the sketch over my bench." In just six weeks, they had the motor on the block testing its power. A marvel of lightness and efficiency, it weighed 179 pounds and generated more than 12 horsepower.

The propellers were much more difficult, since no reliable data on aerial propellers existed. "What at first seemed a simple problem became more complex the longer we studied it," wrote Orville. "With the machine moving forward, the air flying backward, the propellers turning sideways, and nothing standing still, it seemed impossible to find a starting point from which to trace the various simultaneous reactions. . . . Our minds became so obsessed with it that we could do little other work."

During several months of study, experiments, and discussion, Wilbur and Orville filled no less than five notebooks with formulas, diagrams, tables of data, and computations. They were the first to understand that an aerial propeller works like a rotary wing. The same physical laws that produce upward lift when a curved wing slices through the air will also produce forward thrust when a curved propeller blade rotates. Once they had grasped this idea, the Wrights were able to design propeller blades with the right diameter, pitch, and area for their needs.

"Isn't it astonishing that all these secrets have been preserved for so many years just so that we could discover them!!!" Orville told a friend. "Well, our propellers are so different from any that have been used before that they will have to either be a good deal better, or a good deal worse."

They decided to use two propellers turning in opposite directions, so that any twisting effect on the aircraft would be neutralized. The propellers were connected to the motor through a sprocket-and-chain transmission, like the kind used to drive a bicycle. The motor rested on the lower wing, to the right of the pilot, so it would not fall on him in case of a headlong crash. To balance the motor's extra weight, the right wing was 4 inches longer than the left.

In the Wright brothers' gliders, the wing-warping wires had twisted the entire wing up or down. In their new powered machine, the front edge of each wing was fixed rigidly in place. Only the rear outer edges of the wingtips could now be flexed, much like the movements of ailerons on a modern aircraft. The controls were similar to those in the 1902 glider—a padded hip cradle to operate the wing warping and the tail rudder, and a wooden hand lever to control the forward elevator. With a wingspan of just over 40 feet, the new machine was their biggest yet. They called it their first "Flyer."

There wasn't enough space in the bicycle shop workroom to assemble the entire machine. The center section alone was so big that it blocked the passage leading to the front of the shop. When a customer walked in, one of the brothers had to go out a side door and walk around to the front to wait on the customer. They didn't see their Flyer in one piece until the parts were shipped to the Outer Banks and assembled there.

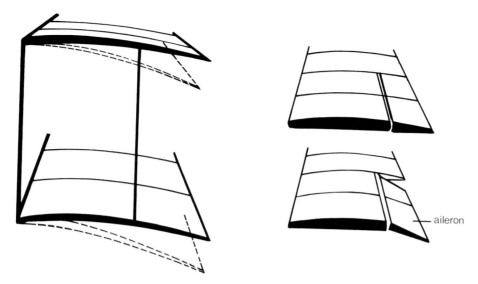

Wing warping in the 1903 Wright Flyer served the same function as ailerons on a modern aircraft.

Wilbur and Orville returned to their camp at Kill Devil Hills on September 25, 1903, and again found a storm-ravaged camp building. They made repairs and put up a second building to use as a workshop for assembling and housing their Flyer. On days with good winds, they took out their old 1902 glider for practice flights. On calm or rainy days, they worked on the new machine indoors.

Their progress was slowed by frustrating problems with the propeller shafts and the transmission sprocket wheels, which kept coming loose as the motor was being tested. Meanwhile, winter arrived early. Rain, snow, and freezing winds buffeted their camp. The water in their washbasin was frozen solid in the morning. They converted an old carbide can into a woodburning stove and piled on the blankets when they went to bed.

"We have no trouble keeping warm at nights," Wilbur wrote home. "In addition to the classifications of last year, to wit, 1, 2, 3 and 4 blanket nights, we now have 5 blanket nights, & 5 blankets & 2 quilts. Next come 5 blankets, 2 quilts & fire; then 5, 2, fire, & hot-water jug. This is as far as we have got so far. Next come the addition of sleeping without undressing, then shoes & hats, and finally overcoats. We intend to be comfortable while we are here."

The Wrights' first powered airplane sits outside the camp buildings at Kill Devil Hills in November, 1903. Wilbur stands in the doorway.

On windy days, the Wright Brothers took out their old 1902 glider for practice flights. The 1903 camp buildings are visible down below.

Orville assembling the 1903 machine in the Flyer's hangar.

The propeller shafts gave them so much trouble that Orville had to go all the way back to Dayton to have new ones made. He was returning to North Carolina on the train when he read a newspaper story about Samuel Pierpont Langley's second and last attempt to launch a man-carrying airplane on December 8, 1903. Once again, the *Great Aerodrome* and its pilot had crashed into the Potomac—and so had the $73,000 Langley had spent on it. So far, the Wrights had spent less than $1,000 on their still untested Flyer.

Orville reached Kill Devil Hills with the new propeller shafts on December 11. The brothers were anxious to test their Flyer before the weather got any worse. To launch the machine, they had built a movable starting track—a 60-foot-long wooden rail made of four 15-foot sections. The top of the rail was covered with a thin metal strip. For takeoff, the Flyer would be placed over this track with its landing skids resting on a small two-wheeled dolly, or "truck" as the Wrights called it, which ran freely along the rail. When the propellers started to turn, the Flyer would ride down the monorail on its truck, heading into the wind until it gained enough airspeed to lift off and fly. The Wrights called this starting track their "Grand Junction Railroad."

They were ready for their first trial on Monday, December 14, but the wind that day wasn't strong enough to permit a launching from level ground. Instead of waiting any longer, they decided to try a downhill launching from the side of Big Kill Devil Hill.

They hoisted a red signal flag to the top of a pole, alerting the lifesaving station a mile away. Before long, five men, two small boys, and a dog came trudging up the beach. The lifesavers had agreed to act as witnesses and help move more than 700 pounds of flying machine over the sand.

Everyone pitched in. Balancing the Flyer by hand, they rolled it along the starting rail, moving each 15-foot section of track from the rear to the front as they went along. When they reached the bottom of Big Hill, the entire 60-foot track was laid on the hillside. Then the Flyer was pulled up the rail and placed in position. "With the slope of the track, the thrust of the propellers, and the machine starting directly into the wind, we did not anticipate any trouble in getting up flying speed on the 60 foot monorail track," Orville recalled.

The Flyer sits atop its movable 60-foot starting track.

The crew of the U.S. Life Saving Station at Kill Devil Hills, located about a mile from the Wrights' camp. These men became the world's first aircraft ground crew.

They started the motor. The propellers turned over, paddling loudly. The transmission chains clattered. The motor popped and coughed, and the whole machine seemed to shudder and shake. The two small boys took one look, backed away, and went racing across the sand dunes with the dog at their heels.

Wilbur and Orville tossed a coin to decide who should try first. Wilbur won. He lay down on the lower wing, sliding his hips into the padded wing-warping cradle. Orville took a position at one of the wings to help balance the machine as it roared down the starting track. Then Wilbur loosened the restraining rope that held the Flyer in place. The machine shot down the track with such speed that Orville was left behind, gasping for breath.

After a 35- to 40-foot run, the Flyer lifted up from the rail. Once in the air, Wilbur tried to point the machine up at too steep an angle. It climbed a few feet, stalled, settled backward, and smashed into the sand on its left wing. Orville's stopwatch showed that the Flyer had flown for just 3½ seconds.

Wilbur wasn't hurt, but it took two days to repair the damage to the Flyer. They were ready to try again on Thursday, December 17, 1903.

They woke up that morning to freezing temperatures and a blustery 27-mile-an-hour wind. Puddles of rainwater in the sand hollows around their camp were crusted with ice. They spent the early part of the morning indoors, hoping the wind would die down a little. At 10 o'clock, with the wind as brisk as ever, they decided to attempt a flight. "The conditions were very unfavorable," wrote Wilbur. "Nevertheless, as we had set our minds on being home by Christmas, we determined to go ahead."

They hoisted the signal flag to summon the lifesavers. Then, in the biting wind, they laid down all four sections of the starting track on a level stretch of sand just below their camp. They had to go inside frequently to warm their hands by the carbide-can stove.

By the time the starting track was in place, five witnesses had shown up—four men from the lifesaving station and a teenage boy from the nearby village of Nags Head. They helped haul the Flyer over to the launching site.

Now it was Orville's turn at the controls. First he set up his big box camera, focused on a point near the end of the track, and inserted a glass-plate negative. Then he placed the rubber bulb that tripped the shutter in the big

Wilbur in the damaged Flyer after his unsuccessful trial on December 14. His hand still grips the wooden control lever.

hand of John Daniels, one of the lifesaving men, and asked him to squeeze the bulb just as the Flyer took off.

The brothers shook hands. "We couldn't help but notice how they held onto each other's hand," one of the lifesavers recalled, "sort of like two folks parting who weren't sure they'd ever see one another again."

Orville took the pilot's position, his hips in the wing-warping cradle, the toes of his shoes hooked over a small supporting rack behind him. Like his brother, he was wearing a dark suit, a stiff collar, a necktie, and a cap. Wilbur turned to the lifesaving men and told them "not to look so sad, but to . . . laugh and holler and clap . . . and try to cheer Orville up when he started."

"After running the motor a few minutes to heat it up," Orville recalled, "I released the wire that held the machine to the track, and the machine started forward into the wind. Wilbur ran at the side of the machine, holding the wing to balance it on the track. Unlike the start on the 14th, made in a calm, the machine, facing a 27-mile-per-hour wind, started very slowly. Wilbur was able to stay with it till it lifted from the track after a forty-foot run. [John] snapped the camera for us, taking a picture just as the machine had reached the end of the track and had risen to a height of about two feet."

Wilbur had just let go of the wing when John Daniels tripped the shutter. The lifesavers broke into a ragged cheer. The Flyer was flying!

Orville couldn't hear them. He hung on to the control lever and stared straight ahead as the icy wind whistled past his ears and the motor clattered beside him. Buffeted by gusts, the Flyer lurched forward like a drunken bird. "The course of the flight up and down was exceedingly erratic," wrote Orville, "partly due to the irregularity of the air, and partly to lack of experience in handling this machine. . . . As a result the machine would rise suddenly to about ten feet, and then as suddenly dart for the ground. A sudden dart when a little over a hundred feet from the end of the track, or a little over 120 feet from the point at which it rose into the air, ended the flight. . . .

"This flight lasted only 12 seconds, but it was nevertheless the first in the history of the world in which a machine carrying a man had raised itself by its own power into the air in full flight, had sailed forward without reduction of speed, and had finally landed at a point as high as that from which it had started."

It had happened so quickly. A boy could have thrown a ball as far as the Flyer had flown. But the Wright brothers were elated. Seven years after Otto Lilienthal's fatal crash, four and a half years after Wilbur's letter to the Smithsonian Institution, they had launched a flying machine that could actually fly.

The group hauled the Flyer back to the starting track. By now everyone was so chilled, they had to go inside the camp building to huddle around the stove.

Wilbur and Orville made three more flights that windswept December morning, taking turns at the controls. The longest flight of the day took place at noon, when Wilbur covered a ground distance of 852 feet in 59 seconds. They were getting ready to try again when a powerful gust of wind struck the machine and began to turn it over.

"Everybody made a rush for it," wrote Orville. "Wilbur, who was at one end, seized it in front, Mr. Daniels and I, who were behind, tried to stop it by holding to the rear uprights. All our efforts were vain. The machine rolled over and over.

"Daniels, who had retained his grip, was carried along with it, and was thrown about head over heels inside the machine. Fortunately he was not seriously injured, though badly bruised in falling about against the motor, chain guides, etc."

For the rest of his life, John Daniels would boast that he had survived the world's first airplane crash. But the Flyer was so damaged that "all possibility of further flights with it for that year were at an end."

Three months earlier, while seeing Wilbur and Orville off at the Dayton train station, Bishop Milton Wright had given his sons a dollar to cover the cost of sending a telegram as soon as their Flyer made a successful flight. Now was the time. That afternoon the brothers walked 4 miles up the beach to the Weather Bureau station at Kitty Hawk and sent a wire to their seventy-four-year-old father, announcing the world's first powered, sustained, and controlled airplane flights.

Form No. 168.

THE WESTERN UNION TELEGRAPH COMPANY.

—— INCORPORATED ——

23,000 OFFICES IN AMERICA.   CABLE SERVICE TO ALL THE WORLD.

This Company **TRANSMITS** and **DELIVERS** messages only o.. conditions limiting its liability, which have been assented to by the sender of the following message.
Errors can be guarded against only by repeating a message back to the sending station for comparison, and the Company will not hold itself liable for errors or delays
in transmission or delivery of **Unrepeated Messages,** beyond the amount of tolls paid thereon, nor in any case where the claim is not presented in writing within sixty days
after the message is filed with the Company for transmission.
This is an **UNREPEATED MESSAGE,** and is delivered by request of the sender, under the conditions named above.
ROBERT C. CLOWRY, President and General Manager.

RECEIVED at   *170*

```
176 C KA CS 33 Paid.      Via Norfolk  Va

Kitty  Hawk N C Dec 17

Bishop M Wright

             7 Hawthorne St


Success four flights thursday  morning  all against twenty one mile

wind started from Level with engine power alone   average speed

through air thirty one miles longest 57 seconds inform  Press

home ~~there~~ Christmas .                    Orevelle Wright      525P
```

This historic telegram was sent from the Kitty Hawk weather station to the weather station at Norfolk, Virginia, then relayed by telephone to the local Western Union office. During transmission, two errors were made: 59 seconds became 57 seconds, and Orville's name was misspelled.

Success: In one of the most famous photographs ever taken, the Wright Flyer takes off on the world's first successful airplane flight at 10:35 a.m. on December 17, 1903. Orville is at the controls, while Wilbur runs alongside. Estimated distance and time: 120 feet in 12 seconds.

*The 1905 Wright Flyer
over Huffman Prairie.*

SEVEN

The First Practical Airplane

After receiving his sons' telegram, Bishop Wright made a statement to the press: "Wilbur is 36, Orville 32, and they are as inseparable as twins. For several years they have read up on aeronautics as a physician would read his books, and they have studied, discussed, and experimented together. Natural workmen, they have invented, constructed, and operated their gliders, and finally their 'Wright Flyer,' jointly, all at their personal expense. About equal credit is due each."

Once back home in Dayton, the brothers issued a press statement of their own: "As winter was already well set in, we should have postponed our trials to a more favorable season, but . . . we were determined, before returning home, to know whether the machine possessed sufficient power to fly, sufficient strength to withstand the shock of landings, and sufficient capacity of control to make flight safe in boisterous winds, as well as in calm air. When these points had been definitely established, we at once packed our goods and returned home, knowing that the age of the flying machine had come at last."

Before their Flyer could be considered a practical invention, the Wrights had to prove that it was capable of more than brief, straight-line flights. That winter they built a new Flyer with a stronger body and a more powerful motor. Now they wanted a flying field closer to home, where they could spend more time testing the machine.

A friend offered the use of Huffman Prairie, the 100-acre cow pasture on the outskirts of Dayton. The brothers immediately set to work on their air-field. First they cut the tall grass with scythes. Then they built a wooden shed in a corner of the meadow. There they assembled their Flyer II in the spring of 1904.

Huffman Prairie had its disadvantages, though. Trees bordering the meadow tended to cut down on the winds necessary for launchings. Cows and horses had to be shooed out of the way before every test flight. "Also the ground is an old swamp and is filled with grassy hummocks some six inches high, so it resembles a prairie-dog town," Wilbur reported. "This makes track-laying slow work."

Their starting track had worked well at Kitty Hawk, but it wasn't as effective at Huffman Prairie, where the bumpy ground made it difficult to lay down the track in the right direction. "While we are getting ready the favorable opportunities slip away, and we are usually up against a rain storm, a dead calm, or a wind blowing at right angles to the track," wrote Wilbur.

The situation improved when they built a new launching device that allowed them to get their Flyer into the air regardless of wind strength and direction. It was a portable derrick—four 20-foot poles forming a pyramid. A 1,600-pound weight was pulled to the top of the derrick and connected to the Flyer by means of ropes and pulleys. When the weight dropped, the Flyer was catapulted along its starting track with enough speed for lift-off.

With this launching system, the Wrights were able to make more than eighty short flights in their 1904 Flyer. Improvement came slowly, however. At first, the airplane was frequently operating out of control. The brothers were still learning to handle the machine, and many flights ended in crash landings as the Flyer bounced across the field and skidded to a stop. They were constantly repairing broken wings, smashed propellers, bent rudders, and splintered skids. They kept a bottle of liniment handy to nurse their bruises and bumps.

With practice their flights grew longer and more reliable. By the end of August, they were making flights of about a quarter of a mile—as far as they could travel in a straight line without crossing the barbed-wire fence separating Huffman Prairie from farmer Stauffer's cornfield. On September 15, Wilbur made his first turn in the air. On September 20, he flew his first complete circle in the sky—the flight witnessed by Amos Root.

The starting track.

When the weight dropped from the top of the derrick, the Flyer was catapulted along the starting track with enough speed for lift-off.

Wilbur and Orville with their 1904 Flyer beside the hangar at Huffman Prairie. The longest flight made by this machine lasted 5 minutes.

After that, the brothers repeatedly flew complete circles. On November 9, in their longest flight of 1904, Wilbur circled Huffman Prairie four times in 5 minutes. Altogether, the Wrights were airborne for about 45 minutes that year.

Their flying practice was often interrupted by foul weather. And even when conditions were ideal, flight tests involved plenty of hard physical work. The Flyer had to be removed sideways from its shed so the tail and forward elevator could be bolted on. Sixty feet of track had to be laid and staked into place, and the 1,600-pound weight hoisted to the top of the starting derrick. After each flight, the 700-pound machine had to be lifted on wheeled supports and hauled back to the starting track across the bumpy meadow.

An electric trolley line ran past Huffman Prairie, and the brothers rode it back and forth between the flying field and Dayton. "I sort of felt sorry for them," recalled a fellow passenger, Luther Beard. "They seemed like well-meaning decent young men. Yet there they were, neglecting their business to waste their time day after day on that ridiculous flying machine. I had an idea they must worry their father."

In the spring of 1905, the brothers completed Flyer III, an improved model of their powered aircraft. The most important change was in the control system. In the earlier Flyers, the tail rudder was linked to the wing-warping system. As a result of their flight experiences, the brothers decided to separate the rudder and warp controls. The pilot's hips remained in the wing-warping cradle, while his hands rested on two levers—one for the elevator in front of the plane, the other for the rudder at the rear. This made the controls more sensitive to the pilot's commands.

That year the Wrights completed more than forty successful flights, spending just over 5 hours in the air. On October 5, Wilbur set a new endurance record when he circled the field thirty times in 39 minutes, covering a distance of 24½ miles.

These flights demonstrated that the Wright Flyer III was the world's first truly practical airplane. It could stay safely in the air as long as the fuel supply lasted. It could bank, turn, circle, and perform figure eights with ease and grace. And it was sturdy enough to withstand repeated takeoffs and landings. Wilbur told a friend: "Our 1905 improvements have given such results as to justify the assertion that flying has been transformed from the realm of scientific problems to that of useful arts."

The 1905 Flyer, considered the world's first truly practical airplane. It set a new endurance record by staying aloft for nearly 39 minutes.

Even so, people weren't easily convinced that the age of flight had arrived. Newspaper accounts of the Wrights' first flights at Kitty Hawk had been wildly exaggerated. To help clear the air, the brothers had invited local reporters to watch the first test flights of Flyer II back in May 1904. Twice that month, reporters had trooped out to Huffman Prairie, and both times, the Flyer's engine had failed before it could lift off. The reporters left and didn't come back. Wilbur and Orville carried out their flight tests with only a few friends and neighbors as witnesses.

By the autumn of 1905, however, word was getting around that a strange winged contraption was circling noisily in the sky above Huffman Prairie. Newspapers in Dayton and Cincinnati began to carry stories about the flights. And yet the news did not go out over the wires. The rest of the world paid little attention to the historic event taking place in an Ohio cow pasture.

People found it hard to believe in airplanes. Understandably so, as Orville stated plainly years later: "I think it was mainly due to the fact that human flight was generally looked upon as an impossibility, and that scarcely anyone believed in it until he actually saw it with his own eyes."

EIGHT

Fliers or Liars?

After their successful flights in 1905, the Wright brothers grounded themselves. For the next two and a half years, they did not fly again or allow anyone to view their machine.

Now that they had built a practical airplane, they wanted to put it on the market. Until their patent rights were secure, they felt that secrecy was important so that no one could steal their invention.

When they offered their Flyer to the U.S. War Department, they were turned down without a hearing. Military officials had already spent a fortune on Samuel Langley's hopeless Aerodrome experiments, and now they were wary of would-be flying-machine inventors. They didn't bother to investigate the Wright brothers' claims.

Wilbur was indignant. "We would be ashamed of ourselves if we had offered our machines to a foreign government without giving our own country a chance at it, but our consciences are clear," he told Octave Chanute. "If the American Government has decided to spend no more money on flying machines till their practical use has been demonstrated in actual service abroad, we are sorry. . . ."

A sunset flight by Wilbur at Le Mans, France.

The Wrights persisted. They looked for other financial backers, and they approached the War Department again. This time they offered to deliver an aircraft that would meet strict army specifications—but first they wanted a contract guaranteeing that the army would purchase their machine if it performed as promised. The army refused to sign a contract without first witnessing demonstration flights, a condition that the Wrights would not accept.

Chanute feared that the brothers would fail to gain recognition for their work. He urged them to fly in public. That would resolve all doubts, he told them. But Wilbur and Orville were determined to protect their interests against rival inventors, who were out to learn all they could. The Wrights would not share their secrets with the world until they had reached an agreement with the army or some other buyer.

They continued to work quietly in Dayton, designing a new version of their airplane called the Wright Type A Flyer. In this model, the pilot would sit upright for the first time. A second seat to his right would accommodate a passenger. A new control system would allow the pilot to operate all controls—the forward elevator, the tail rudder, and the wing warping—by means of two hand levers.

The army, meanwhile, was having second thoughts. At long last, after endless hearings, meetings, and negotiations, the Wrights received a contract from the U.S. Signal Corps. In February 1908, they agreed to deliver a flying machine "capable of carrying two men and sufficient fuel supplies for a flight of 125 miles, with a speed of at least 40 miles an hour." A month later, the brothers signed a second contract with a company that planned to manufacture Wright Flyers in France.

Both contracts called for demonstration flights. Since the brothers hadn't flown for such a long time, they wanted to brush up on their piloting skills and get some experience using their new hand controls. There was no time to waste. That spring they adapted their 1905 Flyer to resemble their new Type A machine. Then they returned to their old camp at Kill Devil Hills for a week of flying practice away from the public's prying eyes.

They hadn't visited the Outer Banks since their historic flights in December 1903. On May 14, 1908, they made history again with the world's first two-passenger airplane flights. Each brother in turn took up Charlie Furnas, a Dayton mechanic who had come along to help out.

The remodeled 1905 Flyer at Kill Devil Hills, May, 1908. This machine made the world's first two-passenger airplane flights.

At the end of May, Wilbur and Orville separated. They went off in different directions, something they hadn't done since beginning their flying experiments. Orville returned to Dayton to start work on a Type A Flyer for the Signal Corps tests, which would take place at an army base near Washington, D.C. Wilbur sailed for France, where he would assemble and demonstrate a second Flyer. He wasn't entirely comfortable about leaving his younger brother on his own. "If at any time Orville is not well, or [is] dissatisfied with the situation at Washington, especially the grounds," Wilbur wrote to his sister, "I wish you would tell me. He may not tell me such things always."

In Europe, Wilbur was greeted with widespread curiosity and suspicion. France had long considered herself the leader in aeronautical research. Many Frenchmen found it hard to believe that the Wright brothers had actually flown at Kitty Hawk as early as 1903. They found it impossible to believe that by 1905, the Wrights could stay in the air for more than half an hour at a time.

The first successful French airplane had struggled aloft in the fall of 1906, flying 726 feet in just under 22 seconds. But no European pilot could stay in the air for a whole minute until 1907.

By the time Wilbur arrived in France in 1908, the Europeans were making rapid progress. Early that year, a French plane had completed Europe's first circular flight. By summer, French aviators had stayed aloft as long as 20 minutes. The French, however, had not yet perfected a system of flight control. Compared to the Wright Flyers, their airplanes were still primitive.

Even so, French planes had flown in public before big crowds, while the Wrights had retreated behind a curtain of secrecy. A Paris newspaper ran an editorial headlined FLIERS OR LIARS? "The Wrights have flown or they have not flown," the editor declared. "They possess a machine or they do not possess one. They are in fact either fliers or liars. It is difficult to fly. It is easy to say, 'We have flown.' "

Wilbur, meanwhile, was having more than his share of troubles. He had arranged to assemble his Flyer at an automobile factory near the city of Le Mans, but when he opened the shipping crates containing the aircraft's parts, he found that many parts had been damaged. It took almost seven weeks to assemble the airframe from the broken bits and pieces that Wilbur pulled from the crates. Then, while he was testing the Flyer's engine, a radiator hose tore loose and sprayed him with boiling water, leaving painful blisters on his left arm and side.

When the Flyer was finally ready, Wilbur announced that he would make his first public flight on August 8 at Les Hunaudières, a small racetrack near Le Mans. A sparse and skeptical crowd, including several prominent French aviators, showed up that afternoon to see what might happen. They watched with interest as the big white Flyer was pulled sideways out of its wooden hangar. Workmen bolted the tail assembly and forward elevator into place. Then they hauled the Flyer over to its starting track and connected it by a rope to the 20-foot-high launching derrick.

Wilbur adjusts the motor of the 1908 Type A Flyer at Le Mans. Between August 1908 and January 1909, he made more than a hundred demonstration flights there, took up sixty passengers, and gained instant fame.

Wilbur with Madame Hart O. Berg, the first woman to fly. The cord around the bottom of Madame Berg's skirt was a precaution against moral hazards.

The plane's propellers were turned over and the motor started its rhythmic popping. Wilbur climbed into the pilot's seat. He was wearing a gray business suit, his usual high starched collar, and a visored cap set backward on his head so it would not blow off.

At Wilbur's signal, the heavy weight hanging from the launching derrick was released. The Flyer started to move along its track, slowly at first, but quickly picking up speed. Then it lifted off, climbed gracefully toward the sky, made two sweeping circles around the racetrack, and glided down for a smooth landing.

The Flyer was in the air for just 1 minute 45 seconds, but the crowd was stunned by Wilbur's easy mastery of the machine. None of the spectators had ever seen a banked turn before. The wobbling flights of French planes seemed crude and awkward by comparison. As the Flyer touched down, the cheering spectators surged out of the grandstand and onto the field to congratulate Wilbur and shake his hand.

"It is a revelation in airplane work," exclaimed the French aviator René Gasnier. "Who can now doubt that the Wrights have done all they claimed? . . . We are as children compared with the Wrights!"

That week Wilbur made several more demonstration flights before enthralled crowds that grew bigger every day. He reported to Orville that "the newspapers and the French aviators went wild with excitement. [Louis] Blériot and [Léon] Delagrange were so excited they could scarcely speak, and [Henry] Kapferer could only gasp and could not talk at all. You would have almost died of laughter if you could have seen them."

At the end of the week, Wilbur was granted permission to use the Camp d'Auvours, a large military ground near Le Mans. From August 21, 1908, to January 2, 1909, he made more than one hundred flights there, captivating France and the rest of the world with his aerial feats.

On sixty of those flights, Wilbur took up passengers. One of the first was Léon Bollée, owner of the French automobile factory where the Flyer had been assembled. The crowd gasped in astonishment as the plane rose from the ground with the bulky Bollée, who weighed 240 pounds, sitting in the passenger seat.

Another passenger, Madame Hart O. Berg, became the first woman to fly. In those Victorian days, it was considered shocking for a woman to show her ankles. So before Madame Berg took off, her husband tied a cord around her skirt, just above her ankles. After she landed, she took a few hobbling steps before the cord was removed. That summer, the hobble skirt became all the rage in the world of ladies' high fashion.

Wilbur's triumphant season in France made him an international celebrity. He lived in the hangar at Camp d'Auvours and slept next to his Flyer, his only companion an adopted stray dog also named Flyer. Soldiers had to be called out to handle the crowds that tried to force their way into the hangar to see Wilbur and his flying machine close up. One woman eluded the soldiers and bored a peephole through the hangar wall. A song called "Il Vole" ("He

Volunteers hauling the launching weight to the top of the derrick.

Flies") became a popular hit in Paris. As flying-machine mania swept through the French capital, bookshops featured a new volume called *Les Premiers Hommes-oiseaux* [*The First Birdmen*]: *Wilbur et Orville Wright*.

Wilbur became well known for something other than his flying skills—his quiet modesty. Once, when asked to make an after-dinner speech at a banquet in his honor, he said jokingly, "I know of only one bird, the parrot, that talks, and it can't fly very high."

Across the Atlantic, Orville was preparing for army acceptance tests of the Wrights' Signal Corps Flyer. Before he could get into the air, however, rivals of the Wright brothers made the first public airplane flights to take place in the United States. On July 4, 1908, Glenn Curtiss flew just over a mile in an airplane built by members of the Aerial Experiment Association. In August, Douglas McCurdy flew 2 miles. But it was Orville's flying in September that brought home to the American public that the age of flight had truly begun.

Wilbur flies triumphantly over Le Mans.

Orville circling the Fort Myer, Virginia, parade ground in the Wrights' 1908 Signal Corps Flyer.

NINE

The Conquering Heroes

Orville began his demonstration flights on September 3, 1908, taking off from the parade ground at Fort Myer, Virginia, as army officers looked on. From the beginning he flew as spectacularly as his brother in France. He set new records almost every day, flying higher and longer than anyone had ever flown.

Soon thousands of spectators were converging on Fort Myer from nearby Washington to watch Orville fly. They were not disappointed. By the end of the first week of trials, he was regularly making flights that lasted an hour or more.

"The newspapers for several days have been full of the stories of your dandy flights," wrote Wilbur from France, "and whereas a week ago I was a marvel of skill, now they do not hesitate to tell me that I am nothing but a 'dud' and that you are the only genuine skyscraper. Such is fame! Your flights have naturally created an immense sensation in Europe and I suppose that America is nearly wild."

As Orville began his third week of test flights, disaster struck. On the afternoon of September 17, he took off with a young Signal Corps officer, Lieutenant Thomas Selfridge, as his passenger. They were making their fourth round of the field when the Flyer's right propeller hit a bracing wire and cracked. "I heard (or felt) a light tapping in the rear of the machine," Orville wrote later. "I suppose it was not over two or three seconds from the time the first taps were heard, till two big thumps, which gave the machine a terrible shaking, showed that something had broken."

Orville cut the motor and tried to land, but the plane went into a nosedive: "Quick as a flash, the machine turned down in front and started straight for the ground. . . . Lieutenant Selfridge up to this time had not uttered a word though he . . . turned once or twice to look into my face. But when the machine turned headfirst for the ground, he exclaimed 'Oh! Oh!' in an almost inaudible voice."

The Flyer hit the parade ground with a sickening thud. Orville and Selfridge were pinned beneath the wreckage, concealed beneath a swirling cloud of dust.

Selfridge's skull was fractured. He died that evening without gaining consciousness—the first person to be killed in the crash of a powered airplane. Orville escaped with a fractured thigh, several broken ribs, severe scalp wounds, and back injuries. When news of the accident reached Dayton, Katharine rushed to Orville's bedside. She stayed in Washington to look after her brother until he was released from the hospital seven weeks later.

The crash interrupted the test flights but did not end them. Having witnessed the Flyer's outstanding performance, the Signal Corps wanted to go ahead with more tests after Orville recovered. "No one who saw the flights of the last few days at Fort Myer could doubt for an instant that the problem of aerial navigation was solved," said an army spokesman. "If Mr. Wright should never again enter an airplane, his work last week at Fort Myer will have secured him a lasting place in history as the man who showed the world that mechanical flight was an assured success."

Wilbur was preparing for a flight at Camp d'Auvours in France when a cablegram arrived informing him of Orville's crash. The message offered few details. It was still too early to tell how badly Orville had been hurt. For a long time Wilbur remained inside the Flyer's hangar without saying a word to anyone. He paced back and forth, twisting a piece of wire in his hands. Finally he announced that he would go into Le Mans, 5 miles away, where further messages would reach him more quickly. He insisted on going by himself. Bent over the handlebars of his bicycle, he disappeared down a tree-lined country lane, alone with his private thoughts.

The crash at Fort Myer that killed Lieutenant Thomas Selfridge and severely injured Orville, September 17, 1908.

In a letter to Katharine, Wilbur blamed himself for Orville's accident: "I cannot help thinking over and over again, 'If I had been there, it would not have happened.' . . . It was not right to leave Orville to undertake such a task alone."

Four days later, Wilbur returned to Camp d'Auvours and set a new endurance record, flying for 1 hour 31 minutes before ten thousand cheering spectators. As he landed and climbed out of the Flyer, he told reporters, "This will cheer Orville up a bit."

In January 1909, when Orville was well enough to travel, he and Katharine sailed across the Atlantic to join Wilbur in France. After a reunion in Paris, the three of them went south to Pau, a popular winter resort at the foot of the Pyrenees. Wilbur trained three French pilots there and flew before a steady procession of notables who came from all over Europe to witness the miracle of flight for themselves.

Recuperating from his injuries, Orville sails for France with his sister Katharine.

Wilbur flies over an oxcart near Pau, France.

Once again, Wilbur insisted on sleeping at the flying field, in the large hangar that had been built especially for his Flyer. His meals were prepared by a French chef selected by the mayor of Pau. He was furnished with a special telephone line that connected the Flyer's hangar to the Hôtel Gassion in Pau, where Orville and Katharine were being pampered in a luxurious suite as guests of the town.

From Pau, Wilbur, Orville, and Katharine moved on to Rome. Wilbur trained two Italian pilots, flew before King Victor Emmanuel and his family, and took up a news cameraman who shot the first motion pictures ever made from an airplane in flight.

Then the Wrights began a triumphant journey home to America, stopping along the way to be honored at banquets and cheered by crowds in Paris, London, New York, and Washington. When the train carrying the conquering heroes pulled up at the depot in Dayton on May 13, thousands of people were waiting to greet them. Church bells rang all over town, factory whistles tooted, cannons boomed out a thirty-gun salute. Wilbur, Orville, and Katharine were ushered into a carriage pulled by four white horses and driven home in glory.

King Edward VII of England meets the Wright brothers and inspects their airplane at Pau, March 17, 1909.

That summer, Orville returned to Fort Myer with a new Signal Corps Flyer for another round of test flights. Wilbur went with him to help out, but they agreed that Orville would do all the flying. Determined that nothing would go wrong this time, they worked slowly and methodically as they prepared their airplane to fly.

"They tinkered and fussed and muttered to themselves from dawn to dusk," recalled Benjamin Foulois, a young Signal Corps lieutenant who would one day become chief of the U.S. Army Air Corps. "It seemed as if they would never say they were ready to go. When you spoke to the two of them, it would be Orville who would answer, and Wilbur would either nod assent or add an incomplete sentence as his way of corroborating what his younger brother had said. At no time did I ever hear either of them render a hasty or ill-considered answer to any question I asked, and sometimes they took so long to reply that I wondered if they had heard me."

The president of the United States, William Howard Taft, and his cabinet were on hand July 27 to watch Orville make the first of two qualifying flights required by the army contract—a two-man flight lasting at least an hour. Orville and his passenger, Lieutenant Frank Lahm, did better than that. They stayed aloft for 1 hour 13 minutes. As they came in for a landing, spectators lining the field began to cheer wildly and automobiles honked their horns in unison. Out in the middle of the field, Wilbur pulled off his cap, waved it in the air, and danced a jig.

Three days later, Orville took off on the second qualifying flight—a 10-mile, two-man, cross-country speed test that would determine the purchase price for the Flyer. The army had agreed to pay $25,000 for the plane if it could average 40 miles an hour. For each full mile an hour over 40, there would be a bonus of $2,500.

To keep the weight of the Flyer down and hopefully increase its speed, Orville picked as his passenger 5-foot-1-inch, 126-pound Lieutenant Foulois. They flew 5 miles from Fort Myer down to Alexandria, Virginia, clattering along just above the treetops. Then they turned around and flew back. "The air was bumpy," Foulois recalled. "It was as if someone on the ground had a string attached to us and would pull it occasionally as they would a kite. But each time Orville would raise the elevators slightly, and we would gain back the lost altitude."

The U.S. Army required that the Signal Corps Flyer be capable of transport by wagon. Here the airplane is being towed by an automobile to Fort Myer for testing.

The round-trip flight lasted 14 minutes 12 seconds at an average speed of 42.58 miles an hour, earning the Wrights an extra $5,000. As the Flyer landed, Wilbur came rushing up to congratulate them. Lieutenant Foulois remarked later that it was the first time he had ever seen Wilbur smile.

By now, the skies over Europe and the United States were beginning to blossom with aviators and airplanes. On July 25, 1909—while Orville was flying at Fort Myer—the French aviator Louis Blériot became the first to fly across the English Channel, piloting a wing-warping plane modeled after the Wright brothers' Flyer.

In August, the first international air races were held at Reims, France. Thirty-eight airplanes, including three built by the Wrights, were registered for the event—though only twenty-three managed to get off the ground. On opening day, spectators jamming the grandstands were treated to the amazing sight of seven airplanes in the sky at the same time.

In Germany, crowds flocked to Tempelhof Field near Berlin to see Orville fly, September, 1909.

Wilbur and Orville were too busy that summer to attend the meet in Reims. Orville was on his way to Germany, where a new company had been formed to build Wright Flyers. Between August 29 and October 15, he flew in Europe for the first time, demonstrating his skill as a pilot before enthusiastic crowds at two fields near Berlin. One of his passengers was the German crown prince, Friedrich Wilhelm, a young man who was passionately interested in flying. When they landed, the excited prince pulled the royal stickpin from his necktie and presented it to Orville. The head of the stickpin formed a crown of rubies with a sparkling diamond *W* in its center—originally for Wilhelm, now for Wright.

Back home, Wilbur was making his first public flights in America. On September 29, as part of the great Hudson-Fulton Celebration in New York City that year, he flew across New York harbor and circled the Statue of Liberty at waist level. On October 4, Wilbur flew up the Hudson River from Governors Island to beyond Grant's Tomb, then turned and flew back—a flight of 20 miles accompanied by a symphony of bells, whistles, and foghorns from hundreds of American and foreign boats and ships that crowded the river and harbor. In case of an emergency landing in the water, a red canoe was suspended beneath the Flyer's white wings.

That one flight was watched by an estimated one million New Yorkers, almost none of whom had ever seen an airplane in the air before.

Wilbur's 20-mile flight up the Hudson River to Grant's Tomb and back was witnessed by a million New Yorkers, October, 1909.

TEN

The Age of Flight

When the Wright brothers built their first experimental kite in 1899, the idea of a man in a flying machine seemed as fantastic as a man in the moon. Ten years later, aviation was a fact of life.

Of course, an aeroplane (as it was spelled back then) was still a tricky thing to fly. Pilots would take off only in daylight, and only if the wind was right. Planes couldn't carry a big enough payload to make passenger or freight flights profitable. There were few permanent landing fields, hangars, or maintenance facilities.

And yet the prospects seemed as limitless as the sky itself. "I firmly believe in the future of the aeroplane for commerce, to carry mail, to carry passengers, perhaps express," Orville declared. "I cannot but believe that we stand at the beginning of a new era, the Age of Flight."

In 1909, Wilbur and Orville established their own company to manufacture Wright Flyers at a factory in Dayton. Orville handled the day-to-day operations of the company. Wilbur spent much of his time in court, fighting bitter and prolonged lawsuits against rival inventors accused of infringing on the Wright brothers' patents.

The Wrights continued to change and improve their Flyers. They added landing wheels in place of skids and moved the forward elevator to the rear of the plane for better control. Some of their planes were designed especially for competition at flying meets and aerial exhibitions, where daredevil pilots

The Wright brothers at the International Aviation Tournament, Belmont Park, New York, October, 1910.

Orville at the controls of the 80-mile-an-hour Wright Baby Grand racer.

risked their lives for thrills and money. The Wright Baby Grand Racer, a single-seater built to set speed and altitude records, was introduced at the 1910 Belmont Park flying meet in New York, the first international air show held in America. With Orville at the controls, the little plane was clocked at the incredible speed of almost 80 miles an hour.

Another Wright Flyer completed America's first coast-to-coast flight in 1911. This plane was called the *Vin Fiz*, after a soft drink that helped sponsor the historic flight. It was flown from Long Island, New York, to Long Beach, California, by Calbraith Rodgers, a 6-foot-4, 200-pound, cigar-puffing pilot who had learned to fly at the Wright Company flying school at Huffman Prairie.

The Vin Fiz *during its historic coast-to-coast flight in 1911.*

Rodgers set out for the West Coast on September 17, accompanied by a special three-car railroad train. One car was equipped as a repair shop and first-aid center, another served as a day coach for newspaper reporters, and the third was a luxurious private Pullman car where Rodgers rested, ate, and slept at night. Along the route, thousands of people turned out to crane their necks and catch a glimpse of the *Vin Fiz* as it passed overhead.

Flying west as wind, weather, and daylight allowed, Rodgers made 70 landings and accumulated a total flying time of 82 hours 4 minutes before reaching his destination on December 10—84 days after leaving Long Island. He flew 4,231 miles, had 12 major accidents, suffered 2 sprained ankles, a twisted back, and a slight concussion, spent several days in the hospital, and kept repairing his airplane and replacing parts as he went along. When he finally landed on the ocean sands at Long Beach, the huge crowd waiting to greet him rushed forward with such enthusiasm that the *Vin Fiz* was pushed back into the surf.

That same autumn, Orville made a return trip to Kitty Hawk. Though the Wrights were now producing advanced models of their powered Flyers, he wanted to test a new unpowered machine and try his hand at gliding once more. Wilbur stayed behind in Dayton to attend to business.

Orville was accompanied by his brother Lorin, Lorin's ten-year-old son Horace, and the British flight pioneer Alexander Ogilvie. They stayed at the old campgrounds at Kill Devil Hills for three weeks in October 1911, and made nearly one hundred successful glides. The new glider, a biplane with a 32-foot wingspan, performed beautifully. On October 24, Orville remained aloft for 9 minutes 45 seconds—a world record for soaring flight that would stand unbeaten for a decade.

Wilbur never had the satisfaction of returning to the wind and sand of the Outer Banks. In 1912 he fell critically ill with typhoid fever, a common disease at that time, spread by contaminated food or water. After battling the disease for four weeks, he lapsed into unconsciousness and died at home on May 30, at the age of forty-five. "A short life, full of consequences," his father wrote in his diary that day.

For the last time, Wilbur Wright was front-page news all over the world. During his funeral, all activities in Dayton stopped. Church bells tolled, automobiles pulled over to the curb, streetcars halted in their tracks, and telephone switchboards refused to accept calls as Wilbur was laid to rest in a

Orville flying his 1911 glider at Kill Devil Hills. Wing warping can be seen clearly in this photo. Orville has pulled back hard on the hand lever to warp the wings, and also applied the full rudder, to initiate a right turn.

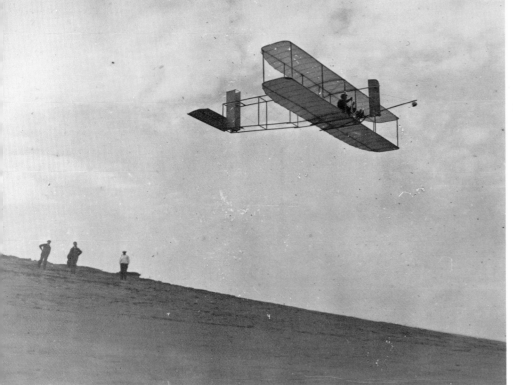

Orville soaring in the 1911 glider during one of his record-breaking flights.

Watching Orville soar.

grave beside his mother's. "Probably Orville and Katharine felt the loss most," wrote Bishop Wright. "They say little."

A spark in Orville seemed to die with Wilbur. In 1915, after most of the patent suits had been resolved to his satisfaction, Orville sold his interest in the Wright Company and retired from the airplane business. He gave up piloting in 1918, but for many years he continued the aeronautical research he had begun with his brother. He developed an automatic pilot system and invented the split-flap airfoil, used on some American dive-bombers during World War II.

A wealthy man, Orville moved with his father and sister to Hawthorn Hill, a lavish mansion on the outskirts of Dayton. He built a fine new experimental laboratory for himself, where he spent much of his time doing what he loved best—tinkering. He made toys for his grandnieces and grandnephews, repaired everything imaginable from clocks to doorbells, and worked long and unsuccessfully trying to perfect an automatic record changer. For his home he designed all sorts of strange labor-saving contrivances, including a vacuum cleaner system built into the walls with hose outlets in every room.

Orville lived to see the airplane transform the world and change people's lives. He saw the first regular airmail service introduced in 1918, the first nonstop transcontinental flight in 1923, the first round-the-world flight in 1924, the first polar flight in 1926, and the first nonstop flight across the Atlantic in 1927. He witnessed two world wars in which the airplane played a critical role. He saw the earth shrink as the jet engine replaced propellers. He lived to see airplanes that flew faster than the speed of sound, and planes whose wings stretched farther than the distance of his first flight at Kitty Hawk.

There were moments when he looked back wistfully to those long-ago days when flying was still a dream that he shared with his brother. He once said, "I got more thrill out of flying before I had ever been in the air at all—while lying in bed thinking how exciting it would be to fly."

Orville died of a heart attack in Dayton at the age of seventy-six on January 30, 1948. Twenty-one years later, in 1969, the American spacecraft

Apollo II made the first manned landing on the moon. As astronaut Neil Armstrong stepped onto the lunar surface, he was carrying with him a piece of the original cotton wing covering from the Wright Flyer that gave birth to the Age of Flight on that windy December morning in 1903.

About the Photographs

The airplane has been called the earliest great invention to be fully documented by photography. Wilbur and Orville Wright wanted to leave a detailed pictorial record of their work. While they were making history as inventors, they were recording that history with a camera.

They took up photography as a hobby, snapping pictures of family, friends, and holiday outings long before they built their first experimental gliders. The wooden shed behind their house served as a well-equipped photographic darkroom.

In 1900, photography became a deliberate part of their aeronautical research. They photographed each phase of their experiments, carefully noting the subject, date, place, camera setting, type of negative, and other details for every picture. Studying the photos helped them to analyze their experiments and learn from their mistakes. Sometimes a photo would reveal phenomena that the pilot and the observers might not otherwise have noticed.

Small handheld cameras using newly introduced roll film had become popular by then, but the Wrights wanted the kind of sharp, precise images that could be provided only by a large view camera. They used two different camera formats—a 4 x 5 inch in 1900 and 1901, and a 5 x 7 inch afterward. Recently improved glass-plate negatives, with an increased sensitivity to light, allowed them to make "instantaneous" photographs. By today's standards, the films they used were slow, requiring an outdoor exposure rarely shorter

The 1902 glider.

than 1/25 of a second. Even so, in many dramatic and beautiful photographs, the Wrights were able to capture their slow-moving flying machines in motion.

As photographers, as in all else, they were partners. Taking turns, they alternated between the roles of pilot and cameraman. They would mount the camera on a tripod, focus the center of the lens on a distant point, and insert the glass-plate negative. The most difficult problem was to snap the shutter at exactly the right moment, catching the moving aircraft within the picture frame.

"The excitement of gliding experiments does not entirely cease with the breaking up of camp," Wilbur remarked. "In the photographic darkroom at home we pass moments as thrilling as any in the field, when the image begins to appear on the plate and it is yet an open question whether we have a picture of a flying machine, or merely a patch of open sky."

Virtually all of the photos taken between 1900 and 1905 were contact printed by Wilbur and Orville themselves in their home photo lab. Usually they made two or more prints from each negative. In 1908, when they began their public demonstrations in Europe and America, there were so many professional and amateur photographers present that the Wrights found it unnecessary to make their own photos. Instead, they were careful to collect and preserve the photos made by others.

They were deeply aware of the historical importance of this photographic record. The Wrights left over three hundred glass-plate negatives and hundreds of prints that record the invention of the airplane. Many of the glass plates were damaged during the disastrous Dayton flood of 1913, when they were submerged in water for several days and suffered from peeling emulsion.

Today the original glass-plate negatives are part of the Wilbur and Orville Wright Collection in the Prints and Photographs Division of the Library of Congress, which also includes several hundred photographs from various sources. The Wright Brothers' Collection at Wright State University in Dayton consists of original prints made from the Wrights' own negatives at the time each photograph was taken. This collection includes prints for which no negative exists, and prints made from negatives subsequently damaged in the Dayton flood. A third major repository of photographs concerning the Wrights and the early history of aeronautics is the Wright Brothers Documentary Research Files, National Air and Space Museum, Smithsonian Institution.

Places to Visit

WRIGHT BROTHERS NATIONAL MEMORIAL, *Kill Devil Hills, North Carolina.* The lonely, windblown campground where the Wright brothers tested their gliders and flew their first powered airplane is now the site of a national memorial that attracted more than 500,000 visitors in 1990. At the summit of Big Kill Devil Hill (its shifting sands stabilized by artificial topsoil and hardy imported grasses) stands an impressive 60-foot granite shaft with feathered wings sculpted into its sides. The aeronautical beacon on top of the monument can be seen for miles in every direction at night. At the foot of the hill is the Visitor Center, which features an informative museum as well as full-sized reproductions of the 1902 glider and the 1903 Flyer I. Nearby are reconstructions of the brothers' camp buildings. A large granite boulder marks the spot where the first powered airplane left the ground, and numbered markers indicate the distance of each of the four flights made that day.

NATIONAL AIR AND SPACE MUSEUM, *Smithsonian Institution, Washington, D.C.* As you walk into the entrance hall of this museum, you see suspended above you the original 1903 Wright Flyer, the first powered airplane to fly successfully. Over the years this historic craft has been assembled, dismantled, and reassembled more than a dozen times. In 1985 it was dismantled one more time and the parts thoroughly cleaned and preserved. The plane was in such amazingly good shape that only the yellowing fabric covering had to be re-

The 1911 glider.

placed. Part of the original 1903 wing covering has survived and is in the museum's collection. Also at the National Air and Space Museum are the 1909 Wright Signal Corps Flyer, the world's first military airplane, and the 1911 Wright *Vin Fiz,* the first airplane to fly across the United States.

AVIATION TRAIL, *Dayton, Ohio.* Maps for this self-guided driving tour are available at the Dayton Convention Center. The route is marked with blue-and-white WRIGHT FLYER signs and includes the two remaining Wright brothers buildings in Dayton—the Wright Cycle Company at 22 S. Williams Street, and Wright & Wright Print Shop at 3rd and Williams Street.

Also in Dayton are CARILLON HISTORICAL PARK, where the Wrights' reconstructed 1905 Flyer III is displayed; and THE UNITED STATES AIR FORCE MUSEUM, the world's oldest and largest military aviation museum, which exhibits a 1909 Wright "B" Flyer.

GREENFIELD VILLAGE, *Dearborn, Michigan.* This complex of historical buildings from around the country was established by Henry Ford as a monument to America's ingenuity and industrial achievement. The last Wright Cycle Shop at 15 North Broadway in Dayton, and the Wright family home at 7 Hawthorn Street, were purchased by Ford in 1936 and moved here the following year. They are open to public viewing along with other structures such as Thomas Edison's Menlo Park, New Jersey, laboratory and Noah Webster's home.

Carrying the 1911 glider.

For Further Reading

The Wright brothers and their achievement have been the subject of several noteworthy biographies and numerous specialized books, popular and technical articles, and scholarly monographs. For this account, I found three recent works especially helpful:

Crouch, Tom D. *The Bishop's Boys: A Life of Wilbur and Orville Wright.* New York: W. W. Norton, 1989. A recognized authority on early aeronautics and the Wright brothers, Crouch emphasizes their family background, their personality traits, and their attitudes toward life and work.

Howard, Fred. *Wilbur and Orville: A Biography of the Wright Brothers.* New York: Alfred A. Knopf, 1987. An informative and highly readable biography, based on solid research.

Jakab, Peter L. *Visions of a Flying Machine: The Wright Brothers and the Process of Invention.* Washington, D.C.: Smithsonian Institution Press, 1990. A unique book that focuses on the Wrights' research and experiments. Jakab offers a detailed technical account of exactly what they accomplished and how they did it.

Other biographies of Wilbur and Orville Wright include:

Combs, Harry, with Martin Caidin. *Kill Devil Hill: Discovering the Secret of the Wright Brothers.* Boston: Houghton Mifflin, 1979.

Walsh, John Evangelist. *One Day at Kitty Hawk: The Untold Story of the Wright Brothers and the Airplane.* New York: Crowell, 1975.

Freudenthal, Elsbeth E. *Flight Into History: The Wright Brothers and the Air Age.* Norman: University of Oklahoma Press, 1949.

Kelly, Fred C. *The Wright Brothers: A Biography Authorized by Orville Wright.* New York: Harcourt Brace, 1943.

McMahon, John R. *The Wright Brothers: Fathers of Flight.* Boston: Little, Brown, 1930.

For the Wright brothers in their own words, see:

Kelly, Fred C., ed. *Miracle at Kitty Hawk: The Letters of Wilbur and Orville Wright.* New York: Farrar, Straus & Young, 1951.

Wescott, Lynanne, and Paula Degen. *Wind and Sand: The Story of the Wright Brothers at Kitty Hawk.* New York: Harry N. Abrams, 1983. A selection of letters accompanied by dramatic prints of many original Wright brothers photographs.

An informative collection of lectures commemorating the seventy-fifth anniversary of the first powered airplane flight was published as: Hallion, Richard P., ed. *The Wright Brothers: Heirs of Prometheus.* Washington, D.C.: Smithsonian Institution Press, 1978. This volume includes Amos I. Root's first eyewitness account of a powered airplane flight, and the text of Orville Wright's 1913 magazine article, "How We Made the First Flight."

An enlightening account of how the Wrights fit in with other American pioneer experimenters in aviation is: Crouch, Tom D. *A Dream of Wings: Americans and the Airplane, 1875–1905.* New York: W. W. Norton, 1981.

Most of the correspondence, notebooks, and diaries relating to the Wrights' invention of the airplane are at the Library of Congress. A collection at Wright State University in Dayton consists largely of material concerning the Wright family and legal documents pertaining to the patenting and sale of the airplane.

Index

(Italicized numbers indicate pages with photographs.)